TRIPPING OVER LOVE ON THE GRINGO TRAIL

CATHY DREYFUSS

Printed in the United States of America
Paperback ISBN: 979-8-218-87501-5
Ebook ISBN: 979-8-218-87502-2

To My Two Mothers

PROLOGUE

There was a window of time, at the tail end of the Sixties, when countless twenty-somethings took off to see the world. We stepped off the traditional path, flung backpacks over our shoulders, and stuck out our thumbs, content to wander without an itinerary or schedule.

One of the routes of this wild world adventure was the Gringo Trail, the trek that took many of us south from the States through Mexico, Central and South America. There were other pathways, as well — hippie trails through India and Europe — but in 1974, I chose Latin America.

This is the story of that journey, an experience that would be impossible to replicate in the modern world. It is a tale of risk taking, shameless behavior, extraordinary teachers, physical challenges, heart openings, and heartbreaks. As a young American woman in one of the poorest places on the planet, I was transformed by the experiences I had there: dance, sex, illness, misunderstanding, betrayals of trust, healing and surrender — all set against a backdrop of herbal remedies, African chants, and complete freedom from intellectual constraints and modern conveniences.

It is a tale about learning to see ordinary things differently. But most of all, it is a tale of love — found, lost, and found again.

CHAPTER 1:

CUMBIA! CUMBIA!

I am transported by the clip-clop hoofbeat rhythm of the *claves* and *timpani*, the slightly off-tune trumpets and flutes, and the half-laughing voices of the Colombian band. I close my eyes and imagine my hips starting to roll, my sandaled feet sliding on the wood-slat floor as I move — step, rock step-step, rock step-step — my shoulders syncopating up and down with my hips. I sniff the breeze, the warm rain-flowered air, and feel my body yielding to the rhythm.

My eyes fly open, and I grab the metal railings of the elliptical stepper to stay upright. I am a seventy-something, somewhat overweight woman wearing stretch workout pants and an overlarge t-shirt, not the twenty-five-year-old girl dancing skin to skin with gorgeous Black Latino men in a funky bar in a hot Ecuadorian beach town.

I step off the machine, music pulsing through the headphones in my ears, and dance around the gym, moving to the music, my hips unleashing the memories, the fire, the craziness.

I am transported back in time and become *La Catalina* once more.

**

I grew up in Los Angeles, in the cocoon of prosperity created after World War II. LA in the Sixties was brimming with growth, new construction, and money. My parents, who came of age during the Depression and World War II, had succeeded in creating wealth and safety and accomplished children. Our nation was at war in Vietnam, but it was far from Beverly Hills, and for kids like me, it was easy not to notice. Even nearby

Watts, a cauldron of racial unrest where the streets were a war zone, seemed a world away. Some of us stepped out of our bubble to burst it open and let in the light and the dirt and the noise. Some of us took off to experience the world, while others left the country in protest and despair. I was one of many twenty-somethings who opted to see the world, setting off with little money, a few good books, a sleeping bag, and an extra pair of jeans, but no plan.

It is almost unthinkable these days that a young girl of twenty-three would take off hitchhiking down to Latin America. The world seems so ominous now. But in reality, the world has always been dangerous; it only seemed more benign because we were more disconnected and less informed. Terrible things — military coups, deadly civil wars, rampant disease and poverty, violence and rape, destruction of the environment — were happening then, just as now.

As the Sixties faded into the rearview mirror and the Seventies began, American kids put Canadian maple leaf decals on their backpacks to disguise themselves as Nixon's drug war raged in Latin America and the war in Vietnam came to its bloody end. A generation of young activists was disappearing in Argentina's Dirty Wars. Chile was reeling from Pinochet's coup and President Salvador Allende's assassination, and the civil war in Guatemala was destroying indigenous Mayan communities. But we knew little about any of that. For us — sheltered and somewhat naïve American young people — it was a time of cheap and easy travel, free education, and little pressure to hurry up and get a job.

It was the perfect time to take off on the Gringo Trail.

CHAPTER 2:

CALL TO ADVENTURE

In 1974, I was living in Berkeley, having graduated from the university the summer before with a useless bachelor's degree in history, a minor in music, shitty LSAT scores, and a talent for cartooning.

I was the consummate Berkeley feminist, plump but strong, riding my bike around town wearing overalls with short-sleeved leotards that allowed my long, dark armpit hair to peek out, no bra, a bike clip on my right pants leg, a red camping kerchief around my neck, and hiking boots on my feet. I was terribly nearsighted and wore thick John Lennon wire-rimmed glasses and no makeup. I rarely drank and never smoked cigarettes, but most days I got high. I vacillated between being macrobiotic and eating my mom's roast chicken, between binging on chocolate chip cookies and taking amphetamine diet pills.

I spent my last summer of classes at UC Berkeley getting stoned and watching the Watergate hearings with my roommates. For the next few months, I worked on and off as a Kelly girl office temp, a sandwich seller for Moveable Feast, and a house cleaner. But mostly I did the political work of the time, publishing feminist journals, passing out leaflets, and organizing abortion rights marches. My love life was not that successful; my sex life was sporadic, detached and not particularly feminist. I was like a confused version of Spiderman: feminist politics by day, casual sex by night. My sexual politics were nowhere near as developed as my progressive politics, and since I could not reconcile the two, I just kept them separate.

I was sexually naïve in high school; I did not date and did not relate to boys very well or easily. I managed to survive my first year at Reed College in Portland, Oregon, with my hymen intact. After dropping out of Reed and returning to Los Angeles, there were a few brief events of sex, random and forgetful. When I first arrived at UC Berkeley the following year, I had a couple of one-night stands and then was sexually assaulted by a cabdriver late one night. I was unharmed but ended up pregnant and had an abortion, all before the end of my first semester. I was nineteen years old.

After that, I retreated from any hope of positive relationships with men. The feminist movement was in full swing at that time, and I happily fell into it, feet first. I felt free from male judgement when I was in women's circles, consciousness-raising groups, feminist women's unions, and female communal houses. I felt safe inside the women's movement, but as soon as I walked out into the world, I fell into a trap of ambivalence. I craved male attention, but the sexual adventures were meaningless and sometimes aggressive. I blew off any possibility of love after a heartbreaking and hurtful rejection by the first guy I slept with more than once and dared to call my boyfriend.

I had come to a standstill in Berkeley. I either had to attend graduate or law school or commit to being an artist, which I was too insecure to do. My political life became a lot less fun after Nixon was reelected, the Symbionese Liberation Army kidnapped Patty Hearst, and the FBI swarmed all over Berkeley looking for them. I watched on live TV as the SLA, including a woman who had been a part of our feminist collective, burned to death when the police firebombed their house in Los Angeles. Clearly it seemed like a good time to leave.

When I left Berkeley, I intended to return and live there forever. I told my pals I would be back in six months, but it was years until I visited, and I never lived there again.

Instead, I went back to LA and got a job as a receptionist for my father and planned the journey to Latin America with my cousin Ellen. Every day, Ellen called me from her switchboard job at a law firm on Grand Avenue to my switchboard job at my father's building on Spring Street. We put a trunk line on between us, staying connected while fielding other calls.

"Bunker Hill East," I would say. "May I help you?"

"Yadda, Bladder and Bunk," she'd say, speaking her joke name of the law firm. We talked about our trip, our getaway south of the border. We had planned to go to Europe, but my friend Danny said I wouldn't learn anything there.

"You should go to Asia or Latin America," he advised.

Danny was a Maoist and quite knowledgeable about third world countries, and I had already been to Europe three times before graduating from high school, anyway, including a six-month adventure my parents took me and my brothers on in 1955 when I was four years old.

"You're probably right," I said. "We should go somewhere more interesting."

Ellen was ten months older than me. She was my double first cousin, daughters of two brothers who married two sisters. We grew up close, though we did not know each other much in high school and college. Our moms were best friends and lived their lives together. Ellen was small and thin, a pixie-faced tomboy with a squinty eye, a "skinny malink" in a family of fat women. She got married after high school and moved into the house she grew up in. In her wedding picture, she has a beehive hairdo and lipstick and a blank expression rather than a face of joy. The photo was of someone else, someone she was playing at the time.

When I came back to LA from Berkeley, Ellen had recently escaped from that boring two-year marriage to the nice, boring guy from Garden Grove in Orange County. She attended college for a bit but got the bug to travel. She would come out as a lesbian after her travel adventure and change her name to Coyote, then years later change her name again to Elia, her Jewish name, but at this time in our lives, she was still Ellen.

I checked out a huge hardbound atlas, like the one I pored over so many times as a kid, from the library and traced our route with my finger. We would head down the main artery of the Gringo Trail, the Pan-American Highway, that runs from the top of Canada down the west coast of the US, through Mexico and Central America to Panama, where the highway stops at the Darién Gap, an unpassable jungle with no roads going through. The highway then picks up again in southern

Colombia and runs through Ecuador, Peru, and Chile, all the way to Tierra del Fuego on the tip of South America.

"I think we can go to Tierra del Fuego and back in six months," Ellen said, neither of us having the slightest idea what we were talking about, how far that really was, or how we would get there, but it seemed a lot more fun than being switchboard operators.

Some people would not think it crazy at all to go on a long backpack adventure when they were twenty-three years old. Those people probably went camping with their families when they were kids or spent summers at sleepaway camps in the Catskills or the Ozarks, or spent a few weeks every summer in a cabin in the Upper Minnesota lake district. Those people probably had Scout badges and started campfires with sticks or went backpacking with friends, pitching tents and cooking on a camp stove.

Those people reading my story will not wonder about what we were planning, or think what my family and friends did, which was, "What the fuck are you thinking?" Those people are probably not Jewish, except maybe the ones who went to the Catskills, but even they slept in cabins on mattresses and ate in cafeterias and flirted with the blouse man. That's Jewish camping. The Jews like me, on the other hand, did *not* go camping with their parents, or do *any* Jewish camping, for that matter.

My parents and my entire *mishpocha* — my extended family — are from New York City, mostly from Brooklyn, and they all moved to Southern California. My mother's idea of camping was sitting in a lawn chair on the strip of grass between the sidewalk and the street, drinking a cup of black Yuban coffee and smoking a Pall Mall while doing the *New York Times* crossword puzzle. My father's idea of family trips was driving with me to the deli and the bagel shop, coming home with a tray of lox and herring, slicing the bagels in five pieces, then serving the nosh by the pool after swimming a few laps. I never understood why my father bothered cutting the bagels in five pieces, since he ate all of them.

My only camping experience was at the "Teenage Beauty Farm" the summer I turned twelve, a fat girls' camp in the Santa Monica mountains. Ellen's camping experience was picnicking in the parking lot of Disneyland before it opened or eating burgers off the grill in some suburban backyard. Prior to 1974, I had only been hiking a few times. The first was on a loop trail in the Colombian River Gorge my first year at Reed College, where my friends and I dropped acid, leading me to believe all trails were loops. This caused a problem on Mount Tamalpais in Marin County the following year, my second hiking experience, when I went with a friend, took acid again, and got very lost when the trail did not end up back at the car.

So when Ellen and I decided to hoist backpacks and travel overland to Tierra del Fuego and back in six months, the proper response was, and still would be, *What the fuck were we thinking?*

CHAPTER 3:

CROSSING THE BORDER
- AUGUST 1974

Our journey was set to begin right after August 12th, my twenty-third birthday. I was too frantic and excited to have a party. The next day, my mother and I drove to Ellen's house in La Habra to get ready. We loaded our backpacks with every imaginable camping item except the most useful, like a camp stove, and tied pots and canteens on the outside hooks. We stuffed the packs with plenty of t-shirts, underwear, warm sweaters and a large bag of bullet-sized O.B. tampons, which were almost confiscated a few months later when the border police in Colombia thought they contained cocaine and kept breaking them open and sniffing them. We brought an Instamatic camera and some film, a couple grand in travelers' checks each, and stuck our passports in belly packs inside our jeans.

We tied bandanas around our necks and got on a bus in Santa Ana. I remember my mother was not exactly cheerful, but she tried not to look too worried, and she didn't cry; neither did my aunt.

"Call as soon as you get to a hotel," my mother instructed. "Call as often as you can, even if you have to call collect."

That meant she was serious. Collect calls were expensive and, in my family, used only in emergencies. I do not remember if our mothers were happy about our journey, afraid for us, or thought we were nuts. What I do remember is both of them standing next to the bus waving goodbye. We waved back and were gone.

As soon as our bus left the station heading south to Tijuana, Ellen brought up the question of Gramma Elsie. Gramma Elsie was our mothers' mother and was sickly. She had diabetes and would die years later at the age of eighty-three. But in 1974, we thought she was going to die at any moment.

"What should we do if Gram dies?" Ellen asked me as we settled into the bus seats. It was an issue, since of course we would want to go back for the funeral but might not be able to get back quickly enough.

"I guess we should go back," I said. "But let's just decide when it happens." It did not happen until eight years later, but the question stayed with us for the whole journey.

Once we got to San Diego and had to change buses, we had such a difficult time moving our way-too-heavy packs — which were rattling with all the pots and canteens hanging on them — that we decided to off-load most of it right there, leaving them on the bus. We pared down the load for what we knew and hoped was going to be a long trip. As we got closer to the border, we saw Border Patrol agents inspecting cars and German Shepherds sniffing around.

"Shit!" Ellen dug into her bag for the package her sister gave her when we left.

"We need to do something with these before we get to the border!"

We proceeded to eat all the magic brownies Ellen's sister had made for our journey, scarfing them up in a panic right then and there, convinced we would be searched and sniffed at the border. It did not occur to us that the Border Patrol was more concerned about people bringing drugs *into* the States, not hippie girls taking pot snacks into Mexico. By the time we crossed into Tijuana, we were so stoned we had no idea where the Mexican bus station was. There we were, nine o'clock at night, two gringas in the middle of seedy downtown Tijuana, with nothing to do but take a deep breath, look around, and ask someone for help. We did that so often throughout our journey that it became our mantra.

We got directions and walked to the bus station down unlighted streets filled with trash and men leering at us from dark alleyways. We loaded our packs on the bus and settled in, riding the bus to Guaymas all night with our backpacks tucked safely under our feet. This made it too uncomfortable to sleep, but we were afraid to put them in the overhead racks because of all the stories of theft we'd heard before we left.

It took me hours on the bus to calm down. The dirt and danger of Tijuana at night and the shock of suddenly not understanding the language was intense. Neither Ellen's minimal high school Spanish nor my years of French and sparse Spanish vocabulary were of any use.

CHAPTER 4:

GUAYMAS

As the sun rose and we finally came down from the brownie high, we arrived in Guaymas. We asked for the cheapest hotel and got it. The room was small, with yellowing wall paint stained with cigarette smoke and a wooden slat floor. We sat across from each other on two creaky iron-framed twin beds, said hello to the scorpion on the wall, gave each other a look of *Jesus, what are we doing?* and burst into tears. We hugged each other, cried till we laughed, and headed for the communal showers and our first full day on the Gringo Trail.

The first person we met when we ventured out was Constadino, a Greek sailor wearing overalls and a sailor hat, who'd been travelling for eight years. He had long, tied-back graying hair and muscular arms tanned from years in the sun. We spent the day with him, speaking various forms of English and Spanish and French and Greek. He was wonderful and smart, a warm hug of a man. In the hotel, we drank tequila and smoked a joint of Colombian. He slept on the floor, too late at night to get back to his ship, and in the morning, we made a plan to meet up later that day.

Guaymas had a slow pace, a small village feeling, with a beautiful beach. It was a very intense and lovely first stop. We met two young men, Salvatore and Gabriel, who took us around town, bought us a fancy lunch, and ended up in our beds. I learned a little bit about dealing with men on this journey, and how easy it is to feel obligated to screw after you've been fed free lobster.

The next day, we found Constadino, and he gave me a deep kiss. I kissed him back.

"That you tell me you wanted to, it is enough, you know. That we say I love you today, it does not matter about tomorrow," he said sweetly. We talked like we were old lovers and said goodbye on the street corner.

Ellen and I left Guaymas that night.

CHAPTER 5:

GUADALAJARA

On the way south, we stopped in Guadalajara, a big city on the edge of Lake Chapala. We met the owner of the fancy resort hotel, a young, rich Mexican in his thirties, with hippy hair and a decadently bored expression. Naturally, I had the hots for him right away and ended up in bed in his hotel room.

In the morning, I was surprised to see Ellen in the next bed with another young man. I hadn't expected that she would be casual about sex. We did not know each other's lives that well at that point, having gone separate ways after high school, and I only knew she married right away.

"El, do you think it's strange that this is not the trip we had planned, getting treated, eating fantastic fish and drinking tall glasses of orange juice? We've paid for only two nights so far. It's a little disturbing, don't you think, like we left our politics behind or something?"

"I suppose," Ellen said. "But hey, this trip is a glide — you go where it takes you."

We spent two weird, empty-feeling days in Guadalajara after the men never came to our hotel to show us around town as promised. I could not help feeling a little lonely and let down, the familiar fallout from one-night stands I had experienced in Berkeley. We spent time in San Juan de Dios Mercado, saw Orozco's murals in the Hospicio orphanage, spent a few hours at Lake Chapala, and planned to leave for Mexico City in the morning. We were invited out to dinner by two well-dressed Mexican businessmen we met at the lake. They seemed harmless enough, especially when they picked us up in a Mercedes.

"*¡Vamos!*" the man in the passenger seat said with a smile as Ellen and I got in the backseat. They made small talk with us as the driver moved onto a main road heading away from the city center.

"*¿De dónde son?*" he asked.

"California," I told him, then asked where we were going in my simple Spanish. "*¿Dónde vamos?*"

Ellen looked at me with fear as we both realized we were headed out of town, far from any restaurant.

"I thought they said dinner?" she whispered, her voice panicked.

"Uh oh. Did we get it wrong? What did they say?"

"Stop the car! *¡Pare!*" Ellen shouted.

"*¿Qué pasa?*" the passenger said, no longer smiling.

Ellen started to grab the door handle, ready to jump.

"Ok, ok," the driver said as he slowed to the curb and turned the car around. They dropped us off at the city center, and we made our way to the hotel.

After that incident, our first priority on the adventure was to learn Spanish. We needed a better grasp of the language so we would not find ourselves kidnapped by lewd men in a Mercedes. We heard that the Spanish language schools in Cuernavaca, a city near the capital, were good and not too expensive, so we added another stop to our unfolding itinerary.

CHAPTER 6:

ANGELINA

Ellen had studied Spanish in high school, and I had eight years of French under my belt, but the only Spanish I knew was what I learned at home. I called it "kitchen Spanish," the basic vocabulary needed to communicate with the long line of Guatemalan housekeepers who came to work in our house in Beverly Hills. First there was Zoila, then Hilda, then Consuela, then Angelina — the oldest of them all. They were cousins, sisters, aunts and nieces who came up from Guatemala, got jobs in our house, took classes in English, got better jobs, and sent for another family member to take their place. I realized later that their presence in my life opened my ears to Spanish and my interest in Latin America.

Angelina was the one I remember best, having stayed with our family the longest, for years after I left home. She was ageless, five-feet tall, stocky and powerful with large, muscular arms and thighs, smooth brown skin and a round stomach. Her face was an Indian face, with a wide forehead, black eyes, high cheekbones and a big smile. Her black wiry hair was pulled back in a bun, with strands of gray in front. I never saw her teeth; she always laughed behind her hand. Her feet splayed flat from wearing sandals all her life and her hands and fingers were strong and wide like a baseball glove. She wore old house dresses or skirts and aprons of different patterns and colors layered one on top of the other, an American version of Guatemalan dress.

Angelina stayed with my parents when they moved to a house in La Habra, the town in Orange County where my other aunts and uncles and cousins lived. My maternal grandparents lived with them downstairs. Angelina took care of my Gramma Elsie, who by that time was in a wheelchair, having lost her leg to diabetes. She lifted my grandmother like she once lifted bales of laundry, as if she were about to hoist her on top of her head and carry her to the river. She could even lift my grandfather Pop-Pop, all two-hundred-and-fifty pounds of him, if necessary, and he knew it. Angelina took care of my mother, who was recovering from thyroid cancer, as well. She waited on my father and my grandfather with equally good nature.

She was like an appliance: sturdy, quiet, ever present and always in the moment, as if she had no past and no present outside of our house. She rarely spoke of her family or her children or her life back home. She just laughed, a belly laugh, smiling behind her hand, embarrassingly covering up her open, giggling mouth.

Angelina never wanted to eat dinner with us, even though she was always invited to do so. Instead, she stood behind the kitchen counter, elbows on the tiles, and laughed at our conversation. We were convinced she understood every word because the timing of her laughter was impeccable. Even the Yiddish jokes of my grandfather got a squeal or a burst at the punch line of the story. It was uncanny and too precise for a coincidence. We were convinced she was a spy.

Years later, when I had returned from Latin America and become immersed in the struggles of the people of Central America, none of it seemed strange, since I had lived within the wide, solid and powerful embrace of Angelina and the other women of her family all those years.

When I first returned home, my mother told me Angelina had gone back to Guatemala and had been out of contact for quite a while. Then, just as suddenly, she reappeared. No one in the family could ask her what happened, since they couldn't understand her Spanish/Quiché dialect. Fortunately, my Spanish was much better by then, and I was finally able to fully communicate with this woman who had been in my life for so long.

I found out that she had a son who had been imprisoned in Guatemala for political reasons. She went back to try to get him out, unsuccessfully, and had walked and ridden on trucks across Mexico before stealing across the California border hidden in the trunk of a car. I tried to picture this woman of fifty or sixty years, with her round mass of skirts and layered blouses, tucked into a trunk. She made it back to our house, saying nothing and asking for nothing, with incredible power and dignity. Shortly after, my grandmother passed away and my parents moved back to Los Angeles, and Angelina left for Guatemala for good. I never found out what happened to her son. Ellen and I planned on looking for her in Guatemala, but we never did.

After my parents divorced a few years later, my brothers and I asked my mother if she missed being married.

"The only thing I miss is my live-in," she replied sardonically.

For her birthday, we bought her a life-sized doll dressed as a housekeeper from Sherwood Galleries in Los Angeles. We dressed her in layers of aprons over her housedress and named her "Angelina." Angelina stood in my mother's condo, and then she inhabited the beach house in Ventura where my mother spent the summers, quietly standing in the corner of the dining room, broom in hand.

After my mother passed away in 2000, Angelina came to live with me and moved with me to all the different places I lived in California, always standing in quiet observation of my life. Angelina could not bend or sit, so instead of sitting in the passenger seat, she traveled in a pickup truck or moving van and spent some time in storage units before being placed in a new home. Eventually, the doll began to show her age. Her cotton tufted hair crumbled, and the nylon wrapping on her face ripped and shredded. My nephew and his wife took possession of Angelina to try to get her repaired. Some twenty-five years after my mother's death, Angelina stands in their garage, partially dismantled, none of us having the heart to throw her away.

One day I showed them a photo I found of my mother, Gramma Elsie, Pop-Pop and the real Angelina, taken in the house in La Habra.

"Who is that next to Gramma?" my nephew asked.

"That's Angelina," I said.

"What? Angelina was a real person?"

They never knew that; they never knew her. They only knew her stand-in, the life-sized stuffed housekeeper always standing in the corner of our lives.

CHAPTER 7:

MEXICO CITY

Ellen and I headed south to Mexico City, a six-hour bus ride from Guadalajara. On the way, we met a nice student on the bus who invited us to stay in his apartment in Mexico City with six other students. The apartment had little furniture or plates, and a bunch of other students crashing on the floor. I felt right at home. These young men were studying to be lawyers, and although they came from small towns, they were sophisticated and well educated. We talked politics, passing joints around and playing American rock music on a boom box. That day, we heard Nixon was pardoned by President Ford for his Watergate crimes. It was expected, but depressing nonetheless, and I was glad to be far away from it all.

We went out to a poorer section of Mexico City to meet Manuel, a friend of a friend in the US. It felt great to speak English again. We went to the *zocalo* — the main square — of three cultures: pyramids, housing projects, and a cathedral, all in one place. Manuel promised us a tour of the city, so we went to his uncle Jorge's typewriter shop. I got into the front passenger seat of Jorge's '54 Chevy, next to Jorge, and Ellen and Manuel got in the back seat. We took off and within minutes Manuel was kissing Ellen.

God damn it. Not again, I thought as the set-up was suddenly revealed. Manuel was putting the make on Ellen, and I was supposed to get together with Jorge. Generosity was not always free, and the scene was becoming all too common and disappointing. Ellen pushed Manuel away and our tour of the city ended right there. Once again, we found ourselves getting out as a car sped away.

One night we went to the zocalo for the fiesta of Independence Day, September 15, with some of the students. In the Metro we saw a portent of things to come: people drenched in confetti with flour on their faces. The zocalo was packed with people — some in costume — food vendors and confetti sellers, lights and firecrackers. Everyone was throwing confetti and flour and cracking each other over the head with eggs filled with baby powder. At first it was fun, but we soon realized gringos were the prime target. We had to walk with our jackets over our faces for protection. Ellen got so much flour in her face she could not open her eyes. It was relentless, scary, and half insane. The guys got a big laugh, but the joke was clearly on us.

There was another side of Mexico City that was not laughable at all. The city was filled with vast slums, houses made of cardboard and tin, and open sewage in the streets. There were lots of vendors selling fruit laid out on pieces of cardboard, and a small girl who could not have been more than five selling peanuts with a baby in a *serape* on her back, another child pulling her pants down and peeing in the gutter.

"What a free, workless childhood we had. I feel kind of guilty," I said to Ellen as we walked through the dirty streets.

"I guess there is no abortion or contraception available to these people, no way to break the cycle of poverty. It is horrendous," Ellen said, sadness in her voice.

After a week in Mexico City, we said our goodbyes, thanked the students for giving us a place to stay and a taste of their crazy city, and got on a bus heading south.

CHAPTER 8:

CUERNAVACA

I was so glad to get out of Mexico City, and we both were in better moods once we finally arrived in Cuernavaca. We found an apartment for ten dollars a week and enrolled in Cemanahuac Institute for a three-week, five-hour-a-day course of intensive Spanish. The first day, we walked the San Francisco-like streets lined with neat adobe houses under a beautiful blue sky. That night we met two young men, one a teacher at another language school and the other a student of music at *Bellas Artes*. Gorge was part Japanese and part Mexican, with almond-shaped eyes and deep brown skin. Timi was blond and fair skinned, eighteen years old, part Swedish and part Mexican. They both grew up in Cuernavaca and invited us to meet their elementary school teacher, an old man who lived in a castle-like house near downtown.

"They don't seem as creepy as the men in Mexico City. Should we do this?"

Ellen nodded, so we agreed to go.

When we got there, we smoked joints and listened to the old man talk about Aztec mysticism and sex. His castle was dark and weird, with Aztec statues, an old phonograph, and a tower to the roof. At one point, Timi and the old man asked me to dance. Timi held me around the waist from behind while the old man in front held my arms tango style. I felt like a ham sandwich, weird and used, with two men gyrating against me, laughing. Timi came in his pants behind me, and the old man did his dance in front. It was a very strange evening. I felt half like flowing with it, half self-conscious and uncomfortable.

"Everything must be cooperative," the old man said.

It was too weird, but I was too stoned to respond. Ellen was sitting nearby on the couch, talking with Gorge and ignoring the scene playing out in the room.

"We need to go home," I said, signaling to her as I broke away from the two men. Gorge and Timi drove us back.

"What the hell was that all about?" Ellen whispered, the only conversation in the car. "That old man was too weird."

She was more guarded than me and would never let herself get into a situation like that. I did not know how to protect myself that well. I was embarrassed by what had happened, yet I still ended up having sex with Timi in the apartment the next afternoon.

We started school and got busy making new friends, mostly from the States. We studied, read, learned to make *chile rellenos, enchiladas,* and fried *plátanos,* plantains cooked either green like potatoes, or ripe and sweet. More than once, we got smashed on tequila in the room, played Ping Pong and pool with the other students, and just generally hung out. We met some other gringo travelers, Mike and Bev and their friend Mike, whose nickname was Big Mike. They were from Colorado, and we all hit it off. They were also heading south down the Gringo Trail, so we hoped to bump into them again along the way.

I became friends with Javier, a student at a nearby college. We spent the night together right before Ellen and I left. He was a sweet boy who told me he loved me but hadn't had the nerve to say it before. I felt like a schmuck, especially since I had just been in bed with one of his friends, Felipe, the night before. Felipe, Black with hippie hair, looked very much like Jimi Hendrix and was another young, eager Latino man I had no hesitation getting into bed with. Maybe it was because it was so easy; there was no risk of rejection, no reason to resist the flattery. I had a difficult time ignoring all the attention I was getting and, frankly, I was enjoying it.

It had not always been so easy. I grew up in a typical Jewish misogynistic household, my mother and I living among men like Indian warriors surrounded by Custer's army. My father and brothers constantly reminded me that I did not meet their fat-phobic body image expectations.

"You're not really going to eat that?" my father would say in a condescending tone as I reached for a second helping of something. He had his
own struggles with weight yet often chided my mother and me about our
eating. My brothers, both older than me and neither very fit nor athletic,
often commented on my fat belly and thighs, sometimes grabbing the
fold of fat around my midriff and laughing. I do not recall ever getting a
compliment from them about my appearance. I was never a sexual being
in their eyes and I spent so many years trying to liberate myself from that
failure, enveloping myself in communities of women while at the same
time seeking sexual attention from men, whatever the cost.

In Mexico I was bombarded with male attention from mostly young
Latino men, and it confused me. I was annoyed and flattered at the same
time. My self-esteem was not that strong, and I did stupid things, like
letting Timi come in his pants pressed against my ass and screwing young
men I had just met. Ellen, on the other hand, had an air of disinterest bor-
dering on disdain towards the constant harassment. She did occasionally
screw some of the men, but mostly she refused to react to the flirtation.

CHAPTER 9:

GUATEMALA

After almost two months in Mexico, we were happy to get away from there and away from Mexican men, and hoped to find a different, less sleazy culture further south. We did have some good times in Mexico, though.

"What were the best things about Mexico?" Ellen asked on the bus ride

south.

"The food, mostly, and some great partying," I said, and she nodded in agreement.

We threw out a list of memories: *pollos* and *licuados*, seafood on the coast, tropical music and dance, playing guitar with the students, *comida corridos* in Mexico City, street food in Cuernavaca, spiked coconut milk on the beach at Lake Chapala, lemon and salt in *cerveza*.

"What were the worst things?" I asked.

"The dirt and the poverty. And the men."

"Agreed," I said.

We took a bus heading south to southern Mexico on the way to Guatemala. We slept for most of the six-hour journey. It was now mid-October, and we had no plans. We heard from other travelers that Oaxaca was a good place to hang out, so off we went.

Oaxaca was overrun with dope-smoking hippies and police raids everywhere, so after spending one night in a youth hostel, we hopped a bus for Tehuantepec, a *puebla* — a small village ruled by women — about three hours south toward the coast. The town bustled with open-air markets and heavyset, strong indigenous women in bright costumes running all the market stalls. It was quite the sight: an entire town with hardly any men around.

After a few hours in the markets eating tortillas and beans from the stalls, we boarded an overnight bus with three crammed to a seat to Quetzaltenango in Guatemala. We arrived as the sun came up, fourteen hours later, after bumping over barely paved roads through gorgeous mountains and jungle and enduring three bus breakdowns. The city was seven thousand feet above sea level in the mountains, chilly and extremely dusty. The difference in the people was incredible. Everyone was helpful and polite, even the men; a welcome change from the attitudes we found in Mexico.

After two more hours on the bus, we landed in Panajachel, a major destination on the Gringo Trail. Filled with tourists, lots of freaks, and campers with license plates from California to Manitoba, it was a lovely village around Lago Atitlán, the most breathtakingly beautiful lake I had ever seen. Lago Atitlán is surrounded by seven volcanoes and is one of the deepest, bluest lakes in the world. The residents of each of the several villages around the lake had their own unique patterned weavings in their *huipiles*, the embroidered tunics the women wore, and rugs. Each village also had a distinct language, not just a different dialect of Quiché. It was a magical place. Many travelers who found their way to Panajachel never left, opening hippie food stores and tie-dye shops, catering to the flow of travelers moving down the Gringo Trail.

We stayed in Panajachel for two weeks and really became part of the scene. Everyone met at the local malt shop, the Hambourgesa, where there were cheap good meals: 75 cents for meat and veggies and great desserts. Lupe rented out rooms in his house for ten bucks a week. He was sort of a hip *Guatamalteco* with three kids and a wife we never saw. Andy from Australia was quiet, seemed a bit gay, and was months into his travels around the world. There were various other crazies, like Clem, an ex-cop from Kentucky who wore hiking boots and women's skirts; Jaime, Lupe's brother, who was getting married to a girl from New York and moving to Long Island; Karen, with plastic fantastic orange hair; and a bunch of blond surfer boys from California, coming up from La Libertad in El Salvador. Then there was Clint from Alabama with a pickup camper, a low-key humor and a fondness for quaaludes and acid. We got to be good friends the last few days. Clint got a kick out of cracking us up when we were stoned, and he surprised the hell out of me by wanting to make love the night before I left. We did it in his truck, of course.

We also ran into Bev and Mike and Big Mike, the friends we met in Cuernavaca. One day we all went to Chichicastenango, where we took some acid and went to the hot springs to soak. It was a powerful experience, beautiful and just right for Ellen's first psychedelic trip. Both Mikes were at least six-feet tall, and on the way back to Panajachel, we walked by an indigenous man and woman, each about four feet tall and carrying astoundingly heavy loads of wood and corn bags. They greeted us politely as they passed.

"*Buenos tardes,*" they said in their thick, guttural Quiché-accented Spanish. "*Buenos* consciousness," we replied.

It was a perfect joke to end a perfect psychedelic day. I knew one thing for damn sure: I had developed a huge crush on Big Mike, and it blew me away when they left. I had so much fun hanging out in our group and had hoped we might stick together for a bit longer, even though I knew it was crazy to make strong attachments when travelling, everyone moving in different directions, in different time. They wanted to hit the Trail down through Central America to get to Colombia by Christmas. Ellen and I did not have any specific schedule or plan, so we said our goodbyes and hoped we would bump into them again.

CHAPTER 10:

CENTRAL AMERICA

We got a ride to Guatemala City from two Americans: Richard, a belligerent, nervous, unlikeable writer from San Francisco who was almost deaf from a bomb in Vietnam where he had been a reporter, and Loretta, a slightly untogether woman from Chicago. We slept under the stars outside a little town in El Salvador, and the next day found a house to rent for a few days in La Libertad, in a tropical setting right on the beach. There were tables under thatched huts and a two-minute walk to the water, all for just a dollar a night.

We stayed with Richard and Loretta for a few days, listening to them arguing — Richard shouting and Loretta crying — until we had enough. We spent a day and night at the hotel next to the Tica bus station in San Salvador, going to the embassy for mail and smoking joints at night with some guys from the hotel: a Costa Rican, two San Salvadoreans, a Black Panamanian, and a Nicaraguan. Then we boarded the bus at 5:00 a.m., met two guys from New York, Eric and Bruce — cousins, too — and made friends with the busload. When we arrived in Managua for the night, it was very spooky, like a ghost town, with open empty lots, rubble everywhere, and only two tall buildings nearby. I found someone who worked at the bus station to get directions.

"*¿Dónde está el centro?*" I asked where the city center was so we could find a hotel.

"*No hay ninguno después del terremoto.*" The man explained that the city center was flattened by the earthquake in 1972, a few years before, and apparently nothing had been done to rebuild or even clean up the rubble. The entire city center was destroyed and would not be rebuilt for another twenty years. Thousands of people died, and hundreds of thousands were displaced. In fact, the failure of the corrupt Somoza regime to respond to this disaster and its theft of international aid money was a main cause of the Nicaraguan revolution in 1979. But Ellen and I had no knowledge of any of that.

We slept in a cheap flophouse next to the bus station that had sheets hung up between cots for privacy and no inside toilets. We were the only women there, and our cots were wedged together between men on either side. Ellen and I slept with all our clothes on, and Ellen never let go of her backpack, hugging it tight against her chest. We left as soon as we could the next day.

We kept on missing Bev and Mike and Big Mike, much to my frustration, leaving them notes as we went, along with notes to other friends, as well, telling them where we were headed. We made plans to meet at certain points along the way, a caravan of travelers putting down tents like a circus. We were a moving community of gringos, communicating by notes pinned on boards at hippie cafés, gringo hotels, embassies and American Express offices, hoping our paths would cross with theirs. The friendships had an intensity born out of the need to jump in quickly and be in the moment, without the luxury of time and history.

After one week of fast travel to San José, the capital of Costa Rica, we decided to go to the Atlantic side of the country. It wasn't like we had a set itinerary, other than the plan to get to Tierra del Fuego and back, a plan that was becoming more and more delusional as the journey progressed. Instead, we went where the flow of travelers on the Gringo Trail went, to places we heard about from other travelers, our plans often changing daily. We heard about the palm-lined beaches of Puerto Limón on the Caribbean, and took a train through incredibly beautiful scenery, from mountains through jungles and on to the coast, on November 17th, Ellen's birthday.

Puerto Limón was a pit and intensely humid, so we searched for a place on the beach and found a free spot in Opy's house. The people there were like Jamaicans, Black descendants of slaves who spoke Carib, a combination of Spanish, English and African dialects. Opy, a gorgeous man in his twenties, spoke Carib to his family and clearer English to us.

He had a powerful gaze, the hugest muscles, and great dope, which he made into a spliff the size of a cigar.

"There is no tobacco in that, is there?" I asked, remembering the only other cigar-size spliff I smoked with some hippies in Oxford where I was doing a summer school abroad program during high school. There'd been tobacco in that one and I'd retched for several hours.

"No, mon," Opy laughed. "Dis here pure ganja!"

The town was tiny, with no electricity, only two stores, families who made dinner on request, and a beautiful Caribbean beach. We had a belated birthday dinner for Ellen at a table right on the sand. We spaced out for two days, smoking great dope with Opy and his friends. Other than the fact that my jeans were shredding, I had clogged ears and a vaginal infection from all the humidity, I was feeling great. A few days on the beach to rest and hang out after a lot of moving around did me wonders.

When we got back to San Jose, we found Bev and Mike and Big Mike at our hotel. After an hour of visa hassling, we found ourselves trucking down to Panama with some of my favorite people.

We spent the day in Panama going up to a mountain village for a bath in the springs and stayed the next night at a beautiful beach called Santa Clara on the Pacific, waking to one of the most amazing dawns I had ever seen, intense reds and oranges filling the sky. All I knew about Panama was the Canal; I had no idea it was such a gorgeous country.

In Panama City, we were hit with a blowout of mixed cultures, the most United States-like place so far, crazy, commercial and bustling. It was intensely humid, and every shop had air conditioning blasting onto the sidewalk. We went from freezing cold to hot and humid every few steps.

Panama was where the Pan-American Highway stopped. There was no way to go overland to Colombia except crossing through the Darién Gap, a dangerous route through the jungle with no roads and no people. Fifty years later, the Darién Gap would become a main migration route for migrants and refugees heading to the United States, something unimaginable at the time we were there.

From Panama City, travelers either got on a boat or a plane, and we all opted to fly. Once again, we said goodbye to Bev, Mike, and Big Mike, who were flying to Bogotá, with a plan to rendezvous in Quito. Ellen and I flew out the next day to Medellín.

It was becoming clear to me that Big Mike was not interested in me. Here was this lovely tall drink of water from Colorado, with cowboy good looks, whom I desperately wanted to sleep with, who had no reciprocal energy toward me. Instead, I found myself easily falling into bed with one young, horny Latino boy after another.

CHAPTER 11:

COLOMBIA

We sped through Colombia as if in a dream, unable to get our ten-day tourist visas extended, before we crossed the border into Ecuador. I never understood why Colombia was so strict while other countries let tourists in for longer.

Medellín was filled with well-dressed, sophisticated and good-looking men and women who could have been in Paris or New York. We watched a man in a gorgeous suit nip the top off a small mango and in one movement suck out all the juice, without leaving a drop on his face or suit.

"That looks easy," I said to Ellen as we purchased a few small mangos at a fruit stand. It looked easy but it wasn't. We bit off the tip and squeezed the mangos into our mouths, splattering mango juice all over our faces and sweaters.

We left Medellín for Manizales with our friends Greg and Janet, whom we met in Panajachel. Manizales was colder and built on a ridge overlooking an incredible valley. The bus ride took forever, but there was the clearest, biggest full moon I had ever seen, and I realized how much of the wonders of the earth and sky I missed out on living in big cities, where I rarely saw stars or clear, clean water. It was Thanksgiving back home, but I did not feel homesick. I was not in a rush to go back, not when every day was another day filled with wonder.

We found a *pensión* for 70 cents a night and spent a day around town. The next day we hiked to Chinchiná along the paved highway, twenty-two kilometers, about ten miles, and practically killed ourselves. Well worth it, but we learned for sure our packs were not meant for long-distance hiking. Besides, Greg was an ex-Marine drill instructor, which explains why I felt like we were on a forced training hike.

The following day we said our goodbyes and Ellen and I hitched a ride in a Mercedes with a businessman in a suit, with free lunch included, to Santa Rosa, a small town with thermal baths an hour away. We fell into a great bunch of people, so much like our families it was crazy. Our hotel had a restaurant underneath, and the men who ran it — and old man and two middle-aged men — were warm and generous. We were happily surprised to find out they were Jewish. Their conversations in Spanish and English were dotted with words in Yiddish. Fathers all, they fed us rum and dinner, and the old man scored me two little packets of Colombian dope.

"I no longer indulge," he said. "Psychedelic stuff not for me anymore."

We hit the baths on Monday and sadly said goodbye on Tuesday morning.

"I don't want to leave! I feel so homesick being around a Jewish family again," I whined.

Ellen agreed. "The old man reminds me of Uncle Max. Weird."

"He kind of does," I said. "I wonder how they all ended up here. Their ship must have landed here instead of Ellis Island. Too bad we can't stay longer, but we need to head south."

We got a ride from a new friend to a nearby town and truck rides all the way to Cali, with a free lunch again — one of the best — from an off-duty bus driver who took us into town to a good hotel. We had discovered the fun and ease of hitchhiking, how much more you see and learn, and so we decided to do it when we could. But it was not always that easy. Getting out of Cali, we took a long walk on the road in the tropical sun, one ride in a van that broke down, then a second ride to Popoyán. We started to hitch out the next day, unsuccessfully. We waited on the road for a few hours and ended up taking a bus, then had to double back in the rain because of dirt roads and landslides we could not get through. The whole thing took almost twelve hours, with me in polite conversation for hours with a nun sitting in the next seat.

In Popoyán, we heard from a bunch of gringo travelers in a hippie café about the famous story of Kilometer 9, a legendary spot on the Gringo Trail. One of the hippies, a longhair from Oregon who looked like he had been traveling way too long, told us the story:

"There is a road that leaves from Popoyán up into the surrounding mountains, through a lush landscape of cow pastures. The bus that takes that route picks up gringo hippies in Popoyán, and when the bus arrives at the Kilometer 9 marker, without anyone asking, the bus driver stops and lets the hippies off. There is no actual bus stop, just a marker along a rural road next to a pasture with lots of grazing cows. This pasture, it turns out, has the best psilocybin mushrooms around, which sprout out of cow dung. The bus stops, the hippies get off, the local passengers on the bus laugh behind their hands, and the bus continues up the road to the next villages. Several hours later, the bus returns down the road heading to Popoyán. Again, at Kilometer 9, the bus stops and collects the various stoned hippies lounging around the marker, waiting to board the bus, the passengers shaking their heads at the silliness of the gringos."

"Have you guys been there?" Ellen asked, seeming interested in checking it out. None of the travelers had actually done it. I was tempted, but we were running out of time, since we still had the crazy idea of going all the way to Tierra del Fuego. Besides, I wasn't sure the story wasn't just one of the myths told along the Gringo Trail.

CHAPTER 12:

ECUADOR

In Ipiales, our last night in Colombia near the border of Ecuador, it was so freezing we spent the whole evening in bed, fully dressed and bundled inside our sleeping bags. The next day we crossed the border to Tulcán, where we got a bus to Ibarra, in the Sierra of Ecuador, up in the Andes mountains. The scenery was spectacular again: deep gorges, a windy cobblestone highway, snow-capped mountains with green patches up the sides, and a dazzling blue sky.

The bus was filled with local women carrying bags and boxes of stuff they bought in Colombia, which was not as expensive as Ecuador. At one point, a couple of women asked us if we could put some of their bags under our seats, as they had their children with them and it was too crowded in their seats.

"*Seguro*," I said. "Of course!" We put our packs in the overhead and draped our legs over their shopping bags. A few minutes later, the bus stopped, and some military policemen boarded. They shouted something unintelligible and came down the aisles searching everyone's seats.

The police passed by us, the only gringos on the bus, without searching.

"*Ladrónes*," one of the women whispered under her breath. Thieves. After the police left the bus and we were on our way, laughter and sighs could be heard. Some women patted us on our shoulders with smiles as they took their packages back to their seats.

"We put the bags with you because they don't search gringas!" one woman told us in the heavily Quechua-accented Spanish of the Sierra. They were cracking down now because of Christmas, she explained, searching for contraband goods from Colombia, stuff like dolls and toys, clothing and plastic kitchenware. She said the police regularly confiscated their purchases for themselves.

"*Son ladrones*," she said.

We were happy to be comrades in arms with the people against the government. Ecuador was under military rule at that time, and northern Ecuador, Tulcán especially, had the most trouble with the government. We found out that the year before there was a two-week *pare*, a general strike, and four citizens and five soldiers had been killed. The man who told us about it had the greatest tone of pride in his voice. The people here were indigenous, so different from Medellín, which was mostly Castilian, whites descended from the Spanish.

We finally arrived in Otavalo, a large bustling market town that looked well off in comparison to Tulcán.

"Everything seems so subdued and soft, friendly and slow here, doesn't it? Maybe we should hang around Otavalo until the big fair on Saturday."

Ellen's idea was a good one. Otavalo was a popular spot along the Gringo Trail, high in the Sierra, with a fabulous craft market. The Otavalan Indian men, the merchant class of the area, dressed in starched white pants and gorgeous deep-blue wool ponchos, and were known around the world.

"Where is everyone right now, all our friends who are travelling around Colombia?" I wondered. "I think we are the first to hit Ecuador."

"That's true," Ellen replied. "It would be great to run into everyone again."

I both looked forward to and worried about my next meeting with Big Mike, hoping I would not act too silly. I needed to let it go and just have a good time.

Otavalo was quiet and pretty, with cobblestone streets, small *tiendas*, little grocery stores, the big market day on Saturday, and lots of *fincas*, small farms, all around. We met two blond cowboys from Utah, and Jose the Portuguese from Canada, and together we hiked to a lake with an island in the middle and stayed there for hours. Ah, wilderness!

CHAPTER 13:

QUITO

The next day we hitchhiked to Quito, the capital city, high up in the Andes at 9,500 feet. Quito had both an old and new section. The poor Mestizos — the mix of Spanish and Indian — and the Serranos — the indigenous people of the Andes — lived up in the old hilly section of the city, with houses of flaking plaster and brick, cobblestoned winding streets, and lots of street vendors. Across town in the flat part of the city, it was rich and new, with one section — Avenida Amazonas — filled with very hip, expensive shops, like the Zona Rosa in Mexico City. The cities in this part of the world seemed set up in the opposite way from Los Angeles, where lots of rich people lived up in the hills and canyons and the poor lived in the flats.

To get to the Hotel Gran Casino, high up a steep hill, we passed open sewers along the streets and saw no sign of electricity or running water, the area too old and steep to modernize. The Hotel Gran Casino was the gringo hotel, a slightly run down, relatively clean, and somewhat safe large hostel filled with foreign travelers. There were two floors of small, windowless rooms off an inside balcony that rented for 80 cents a night.

This is where we met Sara, a blond, big-boned farm girl from Idaho, witty and bright, with a smiling, wide face and deep-blue eyes. She had been traveling with friends who decided to go back home, so she was glad to meet up with other gringas. We latched together immediately, and it was the three of us from then on. We soon became the trifecta not to be messed with. Safety in numbers, we would say, and we hitchhiked with impunity, knowing we were an impenetrable wall of gringa woman power.

We spent Christmas at the Hotel Gran Casino and went to midnight Mass at the cathedral, the first one I had ever attended. It was beautiful and solemn, and it did not matter that I understood so little of the litany, spoken mostly in Latin. There were lots of interesting travelers at the hotel, like Frank, a Jewish writer and philosopher from a noble family of Poland who lived in Canada, and Yuval and Daniel, both Israelis, one a hairdresser for the stars in New York and the other a filmmaker. We spent good times with them, drinking wine on the hill above the city, snorting coke, and talking politics. Yuval and I spent the night together before we all left on our separate ways. He was a very affectionate man; too bad we did not have more time.

We stayed in Quito for ten days, soaking up the Christmas spirit while the city soaked up our money. At a café on Calle García Moreno in the fancy section of downtown Quito, we met the sons of the owners, one of whom was a famous bullfighter named Fabián Mena. He was decked out in a blue suede suit and gold medallions and was incredibly good looking. They paid for our dinner, a nice treat, and invited us to their New Year's Eve party.

"*¡Si mon!* Yes!" we answered. "*¡Vamanos!*"

We spent New Year's Eve with the Menas, riding in a truck with twenty kids, smoking "*punto rojo*" with Fabian. We spent two more evenings filled with music and laughter with some Chilean and Peruvian travelers. Nano, the pretty Chilean, gave us a goodbye kiss before we left to head south.

It was a wonderful way to ring in 1975.

CHAPTER 14:

BAÑOS

We got to the town of Baños, halfway up between the high Andes and the *selva*, the jungle, and a popular stop on the Gringo Trail. It was beautiful and clean, nestled in a valley with huge, lush mountains on all sides, waterfalls and cobblestone streets. The waterfalls came directly out of the mountains, some ice cold and some from thermal pools deep under the mountain, hence the name Baños, "the baths." Concrete bunker-like shower rooms were built into the side of the mountain, with two enormous spigots, one for cold, the other for hot, and huge water pressure. There were lots of gringos there, some of whom seemed very spaced out and burnt out. They came to Baños, like we did, for the water: to shower, wash clothes in the long wooden troughs set up alongside the mountain wall, and soak in the thermal pools. I wanted to stay there forever.

We met two Mormon-looking brothers — clean-shaven, blue-eyed twenty-somethings with short-cropped blond hair — wearing suits with button-down collars and ties. They lived in a fancy house with a Yamaha baby grand piano and electric guitars, smoked powerful dope, and played Chuck Berry. Apparently, they were major coke dealers, contrary to their strait-laced appearances, and had lived in Ecuador for years. I wondered how they got that grand piano over the Andes along those narrow winding roads. Everything about these two was fantastical and odd, but we had a great time playing music with them and dancing in their huge living room with windows looking out onto the volcano.

Ellen and I took our clothes to wash in the troughs, next to the local women dressed in brightly colored weavings, infants strapped to their backs. We had a hell of a time washing our jeans and sweaters with the rough, cheap soap available in the market. It was impossible to get all the soap out, and we laid out everything on rocks to dry in the sun. It took hours, with the sun and the heat coming and going behind the clouds, and when our clothes were finally dry, our jeans were so stiff they stood up by themselves.

CHAPTER 15:

PUYO

Baños was such a wonderful place, and it was great to get our clothes and our bodies clean. We went to the shower bunkers every day and soaked in the thermal pools. It was heaven.

All three of us really wanted to stay for a while, so we spent some time looking for houses to rent. Ellen and I had been traveling on the cheap and everything was so inexpensive that we still had plenty of travelers' checks left. The hotels and *pensiones* we stayed in cost no more than 80 cents a night, and many places we stayed for free. We figured if we could find a house to rent it would not be that much, split three ways. Unfortunately, our search for a place to rent was unsuccessful and we needed to figure out our next steps.

"I really want to see the Amazon. We are so close!" Ellen said.

I took out the *Lonely Planet* guide to South America, now getting crumpled and worn, and studied the map. "I don't think we would be anywhere near the Amazon River, according to this map, but we could get to a tributary river."

"I'm game," Sara said. "We are pretty close, so why not?"

We decided to hitchhike to Puyo, a town along the edge of the Amazon jungle on a small river that flowed to the Napo River and eventually to the Amazon. The three of us — Ellen, Sara and I — stood on the side of the copper-colored, barely paved single-lane road that led from Baños down the mountain to the Napo jungle and stuck out our thumbs. We looked a strange sight, three gringas in jeans and colorful bandanas with camping backpacks and hiking boots. A businessman in a suit picked us up, and as Ellen chatted with him in the front seat, I rolled a joint inside my fanny pack.

"Do you get high? *¿Fumes?*" Ellen asked.

"*¡Cierto!*" he replied. "All the time."

We lit up and passed the joint around. A few minutes passed and the man suddenly drove to the side of the road and stopped. There did not seem to be anything wrong with the car, but apparently the driver was too stoned to drive. There we were, on the side of a jungle road bordered with high, thick bushes, in the middle of nowhere. There were no other cars or trucks in sight.

"*Señor,*" I said in my best Spanish. "*Yo puedo manejar. Tengo licencia.*"

My offer to drive was refused, so we waited. We listened to all the birds and delighted in the colors of the tropical flowering bushes. Every once in a while, we heard a truck coming, and the driver quickly lifted the hood of the car and leaned in, as if he were working on something with the engine. When the trucks stopped and drivers asked if they could help, he would wave them on with "*¡No problema, gracias!*" They drove off wondering, I am sure, what the hell three gringas and a businessman were doing on that road in the first place.

We stayed in that spot for three hours, until the man was clearheaded enough to drive to Puyo. That was the last time we offered a stranger a hit of pot.

The road descended into the sea of jungle that reached out to another vast sea of jungle. Bugs were everywhere and everything was wet as we got lower. Puyo was made of wood, with elevated sidewalks like a town in the cowboy movies, and the whole place was warped and damp. The Ecuadorian jungle was like the Wild West, with outpost towns built by oil companies, towns with names like Shell filled with rugged, muddy-clothed workmen, saloons and unpaved streets.

We waded into the small river that joined the Amazon River miles away, just to say we did, and got the hell out of Dodge as quickly as possible. This time we took a bus.

CHAPTER 16:

PERU AND THE COAST

Sara decided to head back to Baños for a while, and Ellen and I made a pretty quick dash to the Peruvian border to get out of the fucking rain. The climate and terrain changed immediately from heavy wet rain to dry desert heat. It took an entire day to get only a little way after spending two hours standing in the sweltering desert hitchhiking — or trying to — and finally paying two bucks for a taxi to get to Chiclayo, a town on the coast. Two Colombian hipsters we met when we arrived offered to pay for a hotel room at their swanky hotel. We nobly said no and overpaid for a room in a fleabag hotel near the bus station.

The next day, after several hours of unsuccessful hitchhiking, we got a ride to Trujillo, a big town further south along the coast, with a dad and son team from Newport Beach. They had a van complete with air conditioning, a tape deck, and about two hundred tapes. We got stoned and listened to Maria Muldaur while watching the desert of northern Peru out the windows. Unfortunately, the old man was a bigoted creep, his son a bore. These guys were tight, too; they obviously had money but divided checks to the peso and never offered anything. The cigarette pack, which is common property with Latinos, was property only of those in the front seat — not that I smoked, but it was the principle of the thing.

We stopped to look for a place to eat, but the father refused to go to the roadside *comedors*, the little eating places along the road.

"I never eat in places like that. The food is too cheap and probably filled with bacteria. And the service is terrible in these undeveloped countries."

Ellen and I had a laugh about that, thinking of the little kids who were the waiters in these places while their parents did all the cooking.

When we got to Trujillo, we thanked them and quickly split, bumping into a Chilean named Oscar, his friend Pedro the *abogado*, an attorney, and all the rest of their group. We spent the first night on the abogado's office floor, then they treated us to a nice hotel room with good beds, a private bath, and a balcony looking out onto the main drag. We had spent nights in some strange places — train stations, office floors and cheap pensiones — but the hotel room was lovely, and we gratefully stayed four days, dancing in a pitch-black disco with Oscar's friends Enso, Victor and Lorraine. Victor lived in Washington for five years and was getting married to Lorraine, both down here to have a church wedding.

"She is doing a pretty hard thing, marrying a Peruvian," Ellen said after we left them for the evening. "I think it would be difficult to be the wife of a Latino, especially down here."

I did not know how prescient those words would become. We were invited to the wedding, but it was a week away. We left Trujillo to go south and then to the Sierra, saying goodbye to our friends, grateful to have spent some time in their warm and generous company before heading out to the road to stick out our thumbs again.

Outside of Trujillo, we got a ride in a big truck with two long-haul drivers in the cab. Ellen and I sat in the open truck bed on top of burlap bags and metal containers as the truck sped down that stretch of the Pan-American Highway. The highway — two lanes wide and paved, flat and open — ran alongside the ocean, a blacktop ribbon stretching through the enormous desert. The beaches were untouched and empty, the perfect white and golden sand without a footprint, pristine and timeless.

It was the same ocean, the same beaches we grew up on. The surf was so familiar in the way the waves broke, making perfect swells, but no one was surfing. The coastline seemed a mirror image of California, the upside down of the globe. It looked like the Pacific Coast Highway in Malibu, Santa Monica, or Huntington Beach, but devoid of houses, buildings, parking lots, bike paths and piers. It was an eerie joke: here was my perfect beach, but it was too desolate to make me feel safe.

Far off in the distance, we saw the snow-capped peaks of the Andes sitting like cone hats on the horizon and shimmering like a mirage. The mountains are so big and the land between them and the ocean so flat and empty that we were able to see their peaks many thousands of miles away.

As the truck lumbered down the highway, we sat close behind the cab to block the wind, pounding our fists on the cab roof when we needed to stop to pee. Occasionally the truck drivers tossed snacks up into the truck bed, inedible gnarled pieces of deep-fried pork intestines or dangerous looking crunchy balls of grease in plastic bags. Neither of us could stomach them. We sat for hours playing games to distract ourselves from our hunger and sore bones.

"If you could be anywhere at this very moment, where would you be?" I asked.

"In my bed at home. With a good pillow. That's an easy one. What about you?"

"Some comfy couch, somewhere not hot, not dry."

"Good one," Ellen said. "If you could be doing something else at this very moment, what would you be doing?"

"Floating in the swimming pool in the backyard, naked."

We closed our eyes and dreamt of pleasant comforts, good beds and showers, Jacuzzi tubs and big fluffy towels — the dreams of travelers on the road too long, torturing ourselves with sense memories.

I posed the most torturous question of all.

"If you could have anything to eat at this very moment, what would it be?" This sent us into spasms of agony. Eyes closed, we threw out memories.

"Tuna Melts at Hamburger Hamlet, with fries!"

"Fresh lettuce salads with Ranch dressing!"

"Eggs and onions and bagels and lox on Sundays, Rocky Road ice cream with Snyder's Dutch pretzels!"

"A real Coke with ice!" Ellen gave a big sigh at that one. We swayed in reverie of such things, our parched tongues, lips and skin drinking in the tastes and aromas of memory. We played our torture game on and on as the truck bumped and jiggled our sore bodies on the hard corn bags.

"You know what I would really want right now, more than anything?" Ellen said. "A good, ripe piece of honeydew melon. Chilled, preferably."

"Yeah," I sighed. "Oh, yeah."

At that moment the truck took a turn around a bend in the road and slowed as it entered a small town, the highway narrowing as it came through the main street. It was market day, and the road was lined with stalls filled with vegetables and fruit, meats and grains. The smoky smell of corn and pork frying in grease wafted up to us, the cries of vendors selling plátanos, mangos, and *tomates* surrounded us.

The truck pulled to a stop next to the stalls, and as we stood peering over the side of the truck, one of the truckers got out, swung his machete at something and tossed it up to us. It was a big, heavy, green slice of the juiciest, sweetest, most perfect honeydew melon we had ever had.

"Holy shit!" Ellen screamed as she caught the piece of dripping melon. "There was no way they could have heard us. How did they know?"

It was just one of those crazy, magical coincidences that happened on the Gringo Trail. Our truckers dropped us outside of the town before heading east, away from the highway. We thanked them for the ride, and for the melon, and plunged headlong down the Gringo Trail farther into Peru.

CHAPTER 17:

THE ANDES AND MACHU PICCHU

"Why don't we head up to the mountains for a while, get out of this fucking desert? My skin is burning up in this heat."

Ellen's suggestion was a good one, so we decided to go up high into the Andes mountains, some of the tallest, baddest mountains in the world. Their snow-covered peaks offered the promise of cooler air. We had planned to meet up with Sara in Lima in a week, so we had time to see the Andes and get to Lima, then go to Machu Picchu before heading to Bolivia.

After a night in a pensión in Chimbote, a town on the coast south of Trujillo, we got a ride on a huge cargo truck because the buses were full, as usual. The trip to Huaraz, a town in the Andes, was supposed to take eight hours from Chimbote. We left at 8:30 in the morning and did not get to Huaraz until 5:00 a.m., after spending a few hours picking up cargo and passengers, then waiting for the drivers to eat, drink beer, and eat again, then stop and chat until four in the afternoon. We sat the whole time in the back of the open truck, which was getting more crowded as the day went on, on hard burlap bags of corn next to Indians in thick ponchos and alpaca wool hats with ear flaps of colorfully designed embroidery, even though it was so hot our sunburned bodies were dry-roasting.

For several hours the truck lumbered up the winding mountain road, the sound of metal crunching on metal every time the driver shifted gears. When it got dark, the truck pulled off on the side of the road for the night, and the driver went to sleep. It got intensely cold, and we now understood why the other passengers dressed so warmly. We tried to sleep, our wool *ruanas* wrapped around us like mummy bags, but strange lecherous hands kept trying to feel our thighs. At one point, Ellen and I climbed out of the truck to pee, squatting alongside the truck near the edge of the road. It was not until daybreak that we realized there was a sheer cliff right next to the truck, which was parked precariously along the edge of a narrow, barely paved road.

We crashed in a hotel, got stoned, ate chocolate and listened to some men chatting in Quechua outside the window. We had been on the road for almost six months, but we had made it to the Andes. In the late afternoon, we walked along the village path stretching our legs, still in the hiking boots we wore for days on end, wearing heavy ruanas of rough wool over our jeans and sweaters, freezing in the thin dry air. We met an old Indian woman on the mountain path.

"*¿De dónde son usted?*" The woman asked where we were from with a thick Quechuan accent.

"*Los Estados Unidos,*" we answered.

She said she had heard of it. "*Está cerca de Lima, ¿no?*"

Near Lima? Ellen and I glanced at each other. At that moment we knew we were very, very far from home. There were local people walking along doing their tasks; small, brown, dark eyes covered under wool hats. They looked up shyly at us, at our blue eyes and gringa faces and towering height — all five feet, two inches of us.

We turned a corner and stopped dead, stunned as we gazed up at the two peaks, *Blanca* and *Negra*, White and Black. One of snow, the other of night; one of silver, the other coal. The peak called Blanca was on fire from the reflection of the most magnificent sunset we had ever seen. The world was inflamed, and the sky glowed with a warmth and depth that could only be from God.

"Holy shit!" I gasped. "Do you see that? Don't they see this? Why aren't they looking? God has just appeared in the red sunset glow on that mountain!"

People walked by, not looking up, as we stood there, silent in reverence and humility. They seemed so completely oblivious, like nothing out of the ordinary was occurring. I hadn't moved an inch, still standing and staring at the peaks.

"Some people see God every day and don't even realize it, I guess," Ellen said. "Or perhaps they know they are seeing God and live in a constant state of awe."

"I think we are the ones who are oblivious most of the time," I said. "That's why we are in such shock seeing something so extraordinarily beautiful."

The indigenous people there lived this close to God every day and the sun flames bathed them and kept them warm enough, just this side of death and starvation.

**

Sara met up with us in Lima, where we spent one night in a cheap hotel, picked up our mail at the embassy, and left as soon as we could. There had been rumors of a coup attempt that was put down, but now there were armed soldiers patrolling the streets and lorries filled with soldiers with machine guns. We spent a few days in Cusco, recuperating from the truck trip down from Huaraz and the bus and train trip from Lima to Cusco. Travel was difficult, the roads terrible, and seeing armed soldiers on the streets was frightening. We were so bummed by Peru that we almost decided to skip Machu Picchu, but we met a bunch of Brazilian travelers and decided to tag along with them. They were so enthusiastic, colorful and fun, it made us think about going to Brazil.

We all took a train to Aguas Calientes, a town with thermal baths and a train station at the base of the last part of the Inca Trail. The Inca Trail starts in the valley outside of Cusco and usually takes five days to get to Machu Picchu. We slept on the floor of the station and started up the nine-mile hike before dawn. It was a dirt and rock path that ascended and descended until we reached the long, steep rocky steps climbing up to Machu Picchu. I could barely breathe at such a high altitude while carrying my heavy pack, and with the smooth tire tread the shoemaker in Cusco had put on my boots, my feet felt like they were encased in concrete and I could only take a few steps at a time, wheezing for breath. An Andean woman, shorter than me, barefoot, carrying bundles of wood on her back, scurried past me with seemingly little effort while I stood bent over, hands on my knees, trying not to collapse.

When we finally got to the entrance to Machu Picchu, it was still early morning. The fog hung onto the top of the peaks surrounding the ancient site, the sun just beginning to burn through the clouds. We each dropped a pane of acid and got so stoned so fast that Ellen, Sara and I ran up Huayna Picchu mountain so we would not blow it in front of the other tourists. We stayed up there for most of the day. From our mount we could see all of Machu Picchu: jagged granite peaks like wolf teeth ringing the deep cavernous valley filled with stone remnants of the ancient city, everything carpeted in deep green moss. There were stone steps and walls marking what once had been an enormous and vibrant metropolis.

We sat on a flat top of the peak for hours until the sun went behind the western peak and the temperature dropped. It was time to get down, before it was too dark to see the trail. The acid started to wane only a little bit, but we could not wait any longer. I looked down the sheer cliff below the peak and panicked.

"Shit, I have no idea how I am going to get down! Actually, I have no idea how I got up here in the first place!" I laughed as the three of us cautiously started down.

Better to laugh than let the fear take over. Somehow, I slid down in my smooth tread boots, sometimes scooting down on my backside, for once thankful for my fat ass, and we joined the others for the long trek back to Aguas Calientes.

That night we tried to sleep off the acid and headed for the baths at dawn. By 8:00 a.m. we were once more battling to get on the train to Cusco, still crashed out from the experience. Machu Picchu was incredible and worth all the hassle; one could spend weeks crawling around the ruins. But we really had to get the hell out of Peru before we depressed the shit out of each other.

CHAPTER 18:

¡NO HAY!

My memories of Peru are of an unpleasant, cold, harsh landscape filled with unpleasant, cold, harsh people. It was not easy to adapt to the difficulties and inconveniences of a poor country where scarcity was the norm, and many times Ellen and I were struck in the face by the unavailability of things. We got treated badly, ignored, overcharged, and laughed at.

I think the terrain had a lot to do with it. The coast of Peru is a dry desert, and the mountains are jagged and barren, so the people are colder. In Colombia and Ecuador, the land seemed more forgiving, softer and warmer, and so were the people. In Peru there were fewer buses, and they were always full; there were not many private cars, and we rarely got picked up hitchhiking. The *colectivos*, taxis that held several people, were expensive and usually very full. In the cities and towns there was often no electricity during the day, no water at night, and no phones that worked. When we tried to get on buses or trains, we were elbowed and shoved out of the line by big Quechua women wearing bowler hats.

"We have tickets! This isn't fair!" I cried to the ticket agent when we were left on the platform. We learned quickly that fairness had nothing to do with it, and that we could not assume we would get a seat on a train or a bus just because we had a ticket.

"If you want a seat you have to fight for it because there is never enough room, or else you will sleep overnight on the floor of the station," said a gringo sitting on his pack in the station, where we did in fact end up spending the night.

In one town, we went into a dirt-floor comedor with wooden tables and chairs, no glass in the windows, nothing on the walls, and no menus.

Our waiter was a boy about nine years old who came to the table without paper and pencil. This was also quite typical in a place where child labor was the norm.

"I'd like a four-minute boiled egg," Ellen said. "*Un huevo hervido, no más de cuatro minutos.*"

There were no clocks on the wall, and the boy had no watch. The boy stared at us, waiting.

"El, if you ask for a four-minute egg you are going to get a hard-boiled egg. You know that, right? Or just ask for scrambled or fried; that's probably how they usually cook them."

"If they have eggs, why can't I have them cooked like I want? I don't like hard-boiled eggs. I like soft boiled, and I'm not sure what they use to fry the eggs in. Could be pork fat." Ellen could be a bit obstinate at times, and this was one of them. She asked again for a four-minute egg. The boy disappeared for a while and returned with a cooked egg in a bowl. It was hard boiled.

"I told you so," I said as I picked up the egg to peel. Ellen was not going to eat it.

Another time we went into a small tienda, a local grocery store, and saw fresh eggs on the shelf behind the counter where the owner stood. We were staying at a pensión that had a kitchen for us to use, and we were excited by the prospect of a good breakfast.

"*Queremos seis huevos, por favor,*" I said, making my request for eggs in my best Spanish.

"*No hay.* There are no eggs." The man behind the counter scowled.

"*¿Qué quieres decir?* What do you mean? *¿No hay?*"

"*No hay ninguno.*"

"But there are eggs right there!"

"*¡Aquí están!*" I pointed to the shelf filled with eggs.

"*No hay.*" The man wagged his finger at us impatiently.

We left empty handed.

"You know," I said, laughing it off, "it is part of the mystery of this land, the ephemeral nature of things here. You may think you see eggs, but they are not there; it is merely an illusion!"

We were forced to change certain assumptions, like sitting down in a restaurant, looking at the menu, seeing what we wanted, and ordering it. There, even though something was on the menu, it did not mean they had any. When I came back to Los Angeles, I looked at a menu in a restaurant and reflexively asked if they had the item I wanted. The waiter got offended.

"Of course we have it. It's on the menu, isn't it?" he scoffed.

There is a tendency to judge a place like Peru was then as backward, as less "developed," as if the wealth and technological advances make our country a better place to live. We were learning that wasn't always true, that life in Peru and the other places we had experienced was rich and sophisticated in different ways. But we sure missed the conveniences of home and the availability of everything.

"I am so pissed at Peru," I said. "Pissed at the grumpy waiters who give us less food for double the price, cool tea, and watery coffee."

"Yeah, I'm pissed at the sour faces and bad-mannered people," Ellen said. "I'm ready to head to Bolivia. Hopefully people will be friendlier there."

"Perhaps it's our attitude of entitlement that needs to change, if we want to be treated with less hostility." I posited this thought on the way back to our pensión.

"Maybe so," Ellen replied, "but I don't want to stay here any longer to find out."

Ellen and I joked about doing a film with the title of "Peru: The Land of the Scowling Indian." The opening frame would show a grim man with green *coca* slime dripping from his mouth, his lips in a permanent frown, his index finger wagging in our faces. The caption would read: "*No hay*, the mantra of Peru." *No hay*. Translation: There isn't any. No bus, no eggs, no rooms. *No hay*.

Translation: Fuck off, gringas.

CHAPTER 19:

LA PAZ

Ellen, Sara and I traveled by bus and trucks south to Arequipa and then to Puno on the edge of Lake Titicaca, one of the largest lakes in the world. Our last night in Peru was in Puno, and we were ecstatic. We were glad to scram. We lifted our glasses of *pisco*, the rotgut alcohol of the region, and Ellen stood to make a toast.

"So long, Peru! May we never see your grumpy, coked-out face again!"

The next day we were headed to La Paz, hopefully to zip through to Argentina. Somehow, we would get down to Argentina and try our damnedest not to have to go back through Peru on the way back. We crossed Lake Titicaca in a huge canoe filled with stocky muscular men handling the oars and women in heavy ruanas, their infants strapped and bundled against their bosoms. No one had life vests, and the boat was too crowded for comfort. One of the women sat her child on my lap, a heavy four-year-old wrapped in wool. After a while my legs fell asleep, and I squirmed in pain. When I tried to stand up to get the feeling back in my legs, the women screamed at me.

"¡*Siéntate! ¡Siéntate!* Sit down or the boat will tip over!"

I sat and endured the pain and cold and discomfort until we got to the shore. All I remembered of the crossing was the pain in my legs, and the stink of coca leaves and wet wool. We somehow got to La Paz, cold, exhausted and relieved to have made it out of Peru.

La Paz, Bolivia was a real crossroad on the Gringo Trail, a halfway point from where we had been to where we thought we would get to: Tierra Del Fuego, the tip of the continent. It was here we had to decide whether to go farther or turn back. We realized just how far it was to Tierra Del Fuego and how ridiculous we were to think we could get there and back in six months; it had taken us more than six months just to get to La Paz.

The streets of La Paz were layered in dust, the air at 12,000 feet cold, dry, thin. I could not catch my breath. The dust caked my nostrils; the cold dryness sat in my bones. It was freezing, even though February was supposed to be summer. There was no color anywhere except in the ruanas woven with deep red, brown and yellow patterns worn by the barrel-chested Bolivian women. Underneath, the women wore blouses embroidered with red and blue birds. Their black bowler hats sat on top of long braided hair, like a *Stan & Ollie* joke. Their wide skirts, several layers on top of each other like hoop skirts of the prairie, hid their constant pregnancies and covered their bodies when they squatted in the gutters.

The narrow sidewalks were lined with high, cracked adobe walls faded pink and wooden carved doors locked shut, hiding the houses and courtyards and life within. Mestizo men in dark pants, white shirts, and sandaled feet stood in the small box-like shops, the aluminum doors rolled up for the day, while Indian women walked on flat, strong feet up the constant hills, bent over by full baskets on their heads and infants bundled in woven fabric slung on their backs.

When we got to La Paz, the women glanced at us with dark eyes. The children stared, young girls giggled behind their hands, and the old women scowled. I walked in my heavy hiking boots, the wool poncho scratching my skin under the heavy backpack straps, as we labored up the narrow cobblestone streets, with gutters of water and sewage running down the middle, to the gringo hotel on top of the hill. The hotel was like an old whorehouse, with small rooms facing onto inside balconies overlooking the open courtyard. It was cold there, too, with only small space heaters in the rooms. The hotel was not a place to stay, but to pass through, yet gringos of all sorts — Germans, Dutch, Canadians, Americans — stayed for weeks and months, buying, selling, and using the abundant and cheap coke, despite rumors that the hotel was getting dangerous and a bust was imminent. I could see the danger of staying there too long, trapped by the lure of pure cocaine.

**

For the last few weeks that we had traveled after meeting up with Sara, Ellen and Sara had gotten closer, giggling together, sleeping close, and talking intently in quiet conversations I was not invited to be a part of. I tried to navigate the narrow passage between the bombardment of inappropriate and demeaning male attention I craved so badly that I would take it from desperately horny Latino men and my need for true companionship and friendship. The warmth and connection happening between Ellen and Sara was behind a door that was closed to me. I did not understand what was going on between them or why. All I knew was that the trifecta did not feel inclusive anymore and I felt left out.

By the time we arrived in La Paz, my loneliness had reached a level of despair. I knew I could not continue traveling with Ellen and Sara and they did not seem to want me to come along. I decided to leave and head south on my own. I went to the post office to check once more for the possibility of mail before heading off and bumped into Big Mike.

"Mike! Aren't you a sight for sore eyes!"

"Fancy meeting you here!" he replied warmly, giving me a hug. "I've been running around Chile, Brazil and Argentina on my dad's free ticket." Mike's father was an airline pilot, giving Mike the ability to fly all over instead of schlepping on buses and trucks. "I'm on my way back to Ecuador. Is Ellen with you? You two want to go back to Ecuador and meet up with me?"

It did not take me too long to decide. He was a life saver, literally.

"I'd love to meet you in Ecuador. Ellen is here, and we have been traveling with another gringa, Sara, but I decided to split on my own." I only had $400 left from the grand I started out with, but if I was careful, I could spend a good amount of time in Ecuador and Colombia and still fly home. It seemed like the most logical decision, and I was happy about it.

"Great! Let's meet in Baños. I'm flying out in a few days to Quito."

Baños was a good place to hang out and rest and get clean. Hopefully traveling with Mike would be comfortable and we could be friends, whatever happened.

I decided to go to southern Bolivia to see what solo travel would be like before busing through Peru to meet Big Mike. Sucre and Potosi in southern Bolivia were the lovely Spanish capitals of the silver and gold industries of two hundred years ago, and I was looking forward to shopping for weavings and perhaps a little silver.

My head was reeling from the sudden turnaround. For one thing, the trifecta was splitting up, and Ellen and I were not going to be travelling together after months of adventures. I knew I would miss female company: the jokes, the laughing and singing, being *gringas solas* in South America, our party of three and the fun and frolic of women daring the world. The strangest and best thing about the whole decision, once I made it, was that Ellen and I got along much better than before, mainly because I was in a better mood. A load had been lifted off my head and the course of the trip got clearer. We laughed a lot, feeling tighter than we had been in a long time, and talked about meeting up in Colombia to take the trip back home.

CHAPTER 20:

SAN PEDRO

Before I started out on my own, Ellen and Sara and I decided to go on one more adventure together. On our way down the Gringo Trail, we met travelers coming up from the south telling tales of more and more powerful drugs: great weed, *sinsemilla*, *peyote* from the highlands of Mexico, cocaine in Colombia, San Pedro cactus in Bolivia, the mysterious *Ayahuasca* from the jungles of Peru. Our drug intake became more serious the farther we traveled south down the Trail until we found ourselves settled into the grungy gringo hotel in La Paz, snorting absolutely pure cocaine for the first time in our lives. Ayahuasca was not an option. We were told that it was a ritual drug of the Amazonian Indians, and you had to be invited to the ceremony to try it. We knew no one who had been invited to something like that. But we still had to try San Pedro cactus.

One day we followed a few other gringo men onto a bus for a trip to the cactus preserves outside of the city. The bus, as usual, was filled with men, women, children, and caged chickens squawking frantically. When the bus got to the cactus preserve in a vast *altiplano* high desert area, all the gringos got off and began to search for the seven- or nine-sided cacti. When one was found, we gathered around as one of the guys peeled back the layer of strychnine poison with a Swiss army knife. We each took strips of the green, slimy cactus meat that was underneath the poison layer and stuffed it in our mouths, followed immediately by plenty of ripe bananas to help us get it down without gagging. We stayed at the preserve for a few hours, until we finished throwing up and before the psychedelia kicked in too much. Then we wrapped a few more cactus logs in newspaper and got back on the next bus to La Paz.

There we were, gringos in jeans and boots with glassy eyes and flushed cheeks, with the ever-obvious newspaper-wrapped cactus pieces under our arms.

The locals knew what we were up to, and they giggled and mocked us under their hats. I sat next to a man and as the psychedelic took over, I closed my eyes as the waves of nausea came and went. I heard the man talking to himself, or at least I thought I did. He was speaking inside my head, in English no less:

I am afraid to look at those gringos in the face. If I do, I may laugh; they are so hairy and white. They look uncomfortable; the tall men must bend their necks standing in the bus. They tense their shoulders squeezing in, trying so hard not to touch anyone. Strange. 'Buenos,' they say as they dip their heads, nothing more. The three girls with them are wearing pants and boots and ponchos, dressed like men. They stare at us with stark blue eyes, unfocused. One of the girls looks a little sick, her cheeks red, her body swaying back and forth. Her friend, a smaller gringo with a gray ponytail, holds a package under his arm, something wrapped in newspaper, a tube. Ah yes, I know what that is; it is the cactus San Pedro. They have been to the cactus fields and cut some. They probably ate some, too. No wonder she looks sick. Don't they realize these things are not toys to be played with? These strangers come here and take our sacred plants and destroy our lands and destroy themselves. They are fools. Next thing you know they will go looking for Ayahuasca in the jungle and get killed by a poison dart. It will serve them right.

The man was right about the power of San Pedro; it was definitely not something to play with. I was tripping hard all through the night and into the next day.

"That's it for me," I told Ellen and Sara the next day, when we were finally not sick and not stoned and safe in our beds. I told them what the Indian man next to me said about San Pedro. "He gave a warning about Ayahuasca, too. Not sure if I dreamt it or what, but I know we need to respect it. It is sacred."

"No more psychedelic adventures for me down here, either. That was way too intense." Ellen was lying in the bed, eyes closed, still nauseous.

"Quite green around the gills, as my mom used to say," Sara said, pointing at Ellen.

All Ellen could do was nod.

"I think Don Juan was right; these are all sacred plants — *hongos*, peyote, cactus. Not to be messed with."

Ellen closed her eyes again and I lay down on the other bed, glad to be coming down, finally.

Before I left La Paz, I sent a letter to my parents telling them of my plan to go to Ecuador for a bit, and that when I got to Colombia in a few weeks or so, I would head home. I didn't know if Ellen would meet up with me there, since she and Sara were heading further south.

The next day I got on a bus heading south to Oruro and then to Sucre. I was freaked out, excited and a little bit scared, which was a great combo. I said a too-quick goodbye to Ellen and Sara before heading to the bus station.

"You guys better get out of here," I told Ellen before I got on the bus. "It's getting too dangerous."

"We will," Ellen said. "You take care of yourself and get up to meet Mike as soon as you can. We'll leave word at the embassy in Quito once we figure out what we're doing."

"I guess our plan to get to Tierra Del Fuego and back home in six months was a bit delusional." I sighed.

"Completely insane, for sure," Ellen said with a laugh. "What the fuck were we thinking?"

We both laughed at that, the phrase we often repeated like a mantra. We gave each other a long hug, and I ran quickly for the bus, leaving my jacket in the rush. It was sad and sudden, and I cried, although I knew it was working out best for everyone. Now I understood what was happening between them and my feeling of exclusion made sense. Ellen and Sara had fallen in love and seemed really happy and good together.

I was looking forward to warm weather, beaches, the piano in Baños, and crazy Colombia. After a few days in Sucre and Potosi, I planned to return to La Paz for a bit and then hop on a bus for the grueling ride through Peru. I fantasized about a bus equipped with a bed, where I could sleep and dream of grapefruit, and when I awoke, I would be in Ecuador.

CHAPTER 21:

SUCRE

I had no idea when I decided to travel on my own that my journey on the Gringo Trail would take such a wondrous and intense turn. In Judaism, we are asked to contemplate the concept of *T'Shuvah*, the turning, every new year. What are we turning away from and what are we turning toward in the new year? My stepping on the bus was my T'Shuvah. I knew what I was turning away from; what I was turning toward was yet to be revealed.

The bus headed south from La Paz, down a barely paved narrow and winding road across the altiplano high desert. It slowly descended from the 12,000-foot-high capital to the valley below until it arrived in Sucre, a sunny colonial town, before heading south to Potosi. At one point the bus came to a river with no bridge. The river was shallow and wide, and vehicles were usually able to cross it, depending on the season. The bus was filled with passengers, bags, suitcases and supplies, even a few chickens in mesh bags on the roof, but this was the beginning of the wet season, and the river did not look too high. The driver and his assistant got out and chatted in their guttural Andean Spanish, apparently discussing the possibility of crossing. The driver decided to go for it and drove the bus slowly into the water.

When the bus was about ten feet into the river, water rose above the wheel rims and the bus sank a foot or so into the mud. The assistant, a young Mestizo boy, was shouting at the driver, "¡*Dale, dale!* Back up! ¡*No, adelante!* Go forward! ¡*No, pare!* Stop!" The bus dug deeper into the mud with every acceleration and soon it was clear we were stuck. The driver and the assistant and some other men from the bus started taking all the luggage and bags of supplies off the top racks and passed them arms over heads, forming a chain from the bus to the shore.

The men then helped the rest of the passengers off the bus, carrying us from man to man so we would not get our shoes and pants wet because at such high elevation, wet feet could freeze. It was both chivalrous and embarrassing. My body, weighed down with boots, a wool ruana and jeans, was passed from the arms of one man to another until I could jump to dry shore.

After the bus was emptied of its passengers and cargo, we waited at the river's edge for several hours as the men in charge tried to figure out what to do. The passengers — Castilian, Mestizo and Indian — were sitting, standing, and squatting on haunches. And then there was me, a solo *gringa mochilera*, the word for backpacking hippie.

Off a little way from the river's edge, two Andean Indian men stood wearing the traditional conquistador hats, red woven ruanas, tire tread bottomed sandals, and heavy burlap pants cut high above their ankles. They watched the men try to figure out how to get the bus out of the muck and spoke with each other in Quechua, laughing quietly behind their hands, shaking their heads slightly. I imagined they were watching the stupidity of the conquest, five hundred years of Spanish rule, resulting in the Mestizo men driving a fully loaded bus right into the river mud. I was fascinated by the Indian men, by their quiet intelligence and ancient presence. I wondered what they might have thought about me, the only gringo on the bus, as astoundingly different to them as they to me.

There were a Castilian woman and her twenty-something son who lived in Sucre and were traveling to Potosi. They appeared wealthy, the ruling class of old money, and were very kind people. *Durechistas*, or "Rightists," as they called themselves, moved from Argentina in 1952 to escape persecution from the leftist government. We chatted as best we could, and when it became clear we would not make it to Potosi that night but would have to return to Sucre in another bus that was coming for us, the señora invited me to stay in their home.

We arrived at their beautiful three-hundred-fifty-year-old hacienda made of faded pink stucco around an inside courtyard, built by distant relatives who were Spanish silver traders. The adobe walls were chipped, the tiled interior patio floor had floral designs, now scuffed and cracked, and the wooden doors had huge brass doorknobs, the kind opened by large, heavy iron keys. This was a villa of faded elegance, of extraordinary wealth from long ago, now gone. I thought about this woman, obviously well to do, educated, of Spanish ancestry, taking an old bus from La Paz, standing by the river's edge alongside barefoot Indians, laborers and backpacking foreigners, the glory days of her family long past.

The señora showed me to my room, one of a long row of rooms along the side of the inside courtyard, separated from the main house and probably once used for the servants. The room was bare except for a bed and a chair and a small armoire. The bathroom, a concrete block room in a corner of the building, had a tub and toilet. I was grateful for a bath, even more grateful for the toilet and real toilet paper. The typical facilities in this part of South America were a shower head on the wall, a hole in the concrete floor to use both as a toilet and a drain, and squares of newspaper hung from a nail for toilet paper.

The señora had two sons, twins, one of whom was with her on the bus. They were young and good looking. Luis, the one on the bus, was unmarried and the other was married and lived with his wife and the rest of the family at the *hacienda*. The twins were identical and dressed similarly, with no obvious identifying marks to set them apart from each other except for the wife who was with one of them. All during dinner, Luis, the unmarried twin, flirted dangerously with me, igniting the match of my loneliness and lust. By the time we all said our goodnights, Luis and I knew we were not finished with the evening.

He snuck down the corridor and knocked on my door soon after I had gone inside. I could feel the heat already moving in my body as I opened the door. We leapt at the chance for hidden kisses and sex. I don't remember if we even lay down on the bed or merely stayed standing against the wall he pushed me up against when he entered the room. We had a steamy, quick and sexy evening together, barely conversing, and then he left, quietly walking back to the main house.

The next morning, after a lovely hot bath, I joined the family for breakfast in the great dining room. They were sitting around the thick burl-wood slab table on high-backed, carved wooden chairs with worn leather caved-in seats. Both sons were there, and their mother, but the young wife was absent. I looked up briefly at the face of last night's lover and panicked.

Fuck. Is that Luis? I can't tell. There was no recognition in his eyes. *If it is him, he's either a cold bastard or he's trying to hide any connection with me.*

I looked at the other twin, and there was no recognition or eye contact there either. One man was keeping completely cool about our indiscretion, and the other one was not the one. I could feel my heart start to race and my panic grow, along with a rising embarrassment at my dilemma. I had no idea which of my hostess's sons I'd had sex with the night before. I could not tell them apart and neither gave me any hint. Any overt action on my part toward the wrong twin would be a disaster. I sat eating my breakfast, sinking deep into the chair, trying to act as nonchalant as possible, and making small talk with the señora, plotting how quickly I could leave.

I really fucked up this time, I thought. *Here is this wonderful family who gave me a bed and meals and company and warmth. I would have been stranded on the side of the road if they hadn't. And now I need to get out from under the mess I made.*

After breakfast, I thanked the señora and said goodbye to the family and hoisted my backpack for the walk back to the center of Sucre.

CHAPTER 22:

POTOSI

Instead of finding the bus station, I hopped in a truck for Tarabuco, a place I heard had fabulous weavings, before going to Potosi. The locals there wore the same outfits as the two Indian passengers on our bus: karate pants, red woven ponchos, and conquistador helmet-like hats. I could not bring myself to take pictures, as much as I wanted to.

People seemed startled by my being alone, the only gringo in the whole town. But I made friends and had a great lunch from the women in the market and talked briefly and with difficulty to a woman as I admired her weaving. I bought two ruanas, woven ponchos of gorgeous, deep red and blue wool, and put one in my pack and the other one over my sweater.

I spoke a lot of Spanish, especially since I'd started traveling alone, and got compliments on how well I spoke. *If they only knew how little I understand sometimes,* I thought. People spoke Quechua as their primary language and some spoke little or no Spanish with barely intelligible accents. The children, who learned Spanish in school, acted as interpreters between their parents and the gringos like me speaking rudimentary Spanish.

The countryside around there was beautiful, with rolling hills and farmland and the delicious scents of fresh veggies, grasses, mint and flowers. The sky was so blue, and the hills were an intense green. I passed by one small farmhouse sitting next to a field of yellow.

"Do they realize every day how gorgeous their home is?" I conversed with myself, half out loud. "Silly question. Amid beauty all your life, how much do you see every day? It is someone like me who gets blown away by a simple natural and common thing like a beautiful pasture, a herd of goats, and an Indian kid watching them."

I loved the people there and felt happy sitting in the truck, staring back at the ageless woman who smiled at me and laughed with the Tarabuco men as they joked about the gringos. I spent a day in Potosi, cruising the open market, chatting with the vendor women and eating *caldo de pollo*, rice and boiled beans in a little café off the main square. I found a clean pensión for the night and headed to the bus station in the morning after buying some rolls and hard-boiled eggs for the bus ride.

It was a hellish journey back to La Paz. No buses could pass the river, so they were all waiting for low tide. One bus tried to cross and floated downstream a bit amidst cries and shrieks from the crowd of passengers waiting on the road. Not an easy thing, travel in Bolivia. I waited until midnight with the other passengers but finally gave up on the bus and caught the train to Oruro, then waited till 6:00 a.m. and caught a bus to La Paz. Exhausted and dirty, I arrived to the news that Ellen and Sara had never left, but had been toking coke with Tom, the guy from Canada, for a week.

I stayed in La Paz five days, snorting coke and hanging out in the countryside with Ellen and Sara and Tom. Big Mike came over one day, surprised I had not left for Ecuador yet. He came with his friend Francesca, a French woman who was apparently now his girlfriend. I was slightly disappointed, but I got over it. He was flying out to Quito the next day. An assortment of other drugged-out gringos joined us for a few days of fun and frolic, including an all-night party at the Andes Club, playing guitar and enjoying the last moments of all of us together.

I was glad to get a little more time with Ellen and Sara, especially since the last goodbye was so rushed and weird. Then in the morning, I said goodbye to them again before they headed south to Paraguay and Argentina and I went north to Ecuador. They promised me they would leave La Paz as soon as possible, but La Paz was such an easy place to get stuck. The cheap cocaine and cheap food created a dangerous quicksand for gringos. Some weeks later, I got a postcard from them sent to the embassy in Quito. They did get out after I left, and right before the gringo hotel was raided by the Interpol.

After I left La Paz, I was on the bus going from Lake Titicaca in Bolivia to Arequipa, Peru, traveling through vast miles of altiplano ten thousand feet above the sea, where no one and nothing lived except muskrats and insects. It was cold — that particularly dry, thin cold that forces the air out the lungs, sucking out all the moisture. I sat alone in the metal seat, my backpack next to me, my heavy wool poncho covering my only pair of jeans. I wanted to sleep, but the wide women in bowler hats sitting around me chatted among themselves, gossiping in the clicking guttural Quechua language of the Sierra, the putrid odor of chewed coca leaves on their breath.

CHAPTER 23:

THE BUS FROM AREQUIPA & ECUADOR, AGAIN

For months I had traveled through Central America, Colombia, Ecuador, Peru and Bolivia, on trucks and buses, trains and by foot, sometimes sleeping outside but more often in dollar-a-night pensiones. The longer I traveled, the sicker I became with diarrhea, and when my abdomen lit on fire, that fire — unpredictable and overwhelming — demanded to be released. Amoebic dysentery was no joke; it was the main killer of children in these poor countries, and attacked travelers used to cleaner environments with a vengeance.

I took a bus from La Paz to Lima, hoping that my dysentery would back off for the ride. The bus was not what I had dreamed of; there was no bed, and the seats were too hard and uncomfortable for sleep. A few hours into the ride, the fire came on suddenly, fierce and insistent. I gripped my anus tight, holding the fire in, my hemorrhoids heating up like coals.

Can I hold it until we get to Arequipa, I prayed. *Please God, please gods of the Incas, gods of fire, please…*

I looked out through the window caked with years of dirt and grease from countless heads of oily black hair and there was nothing — not a house, store, tree or a bush — to give me a place of privacy. Suddenly I saw a wall, a crumbling piece of an old adobe mud wall, the last remnant of a house or a hut. It stood alone, an eerie monument on a desolate landscape.

"*¡Parase! ¡Parase!* Stop the bus! Stop the bus! *Por favor,* stop the bus!" I screamed and grabbed the metal poles by my seat, pulling myself up and propelling myself toward the front of the bus. As the driver stopped, I flung myself down the metal steps and ran to the wall, heaving my hiking boots through the sand and stones, my poncho billowing behind me. I ran to the wall and squatted behind it, behind the only bit of shelter, of privacy, on this landscape of nothingness.

The bus driver waited. The passengers waited. They knew about the fire, how it burned the insides of the gringos. They had it too sometimes; some lost their babies to it. They waited while I shat the fire out of my body behind a piece of crumbling adobe, cleaning myself as best I could with the pieces of tissue I had stuffed in my pockets. I had no shame, no embarrassment. I had long forgotten to care about such things.

I got back on the bus, curled myself inside my poncho, and leaned my head against the damp rattle of the window as the driver continued to Arequipa.

**

The bus finally arrived in Lima, and I stayed with Tono, a Peruvian man we'd met a few months back. His landlord, an old Italian guy, fed me great spaghetti and talked a mile a minute. I was grateful for a comfortable place to sleep and shower, exhausted by the trip and the dysentery. A few days later, when I felt well enough to venture out, I went to the beach with Tono's friend Osmondo and had a passionate roll-around on the floor of his empty apartment. It was good to be touched again and rub off a little of the horniness. Travelling alone did offer more opportunity for debauchery, and there were always men around, but I was glad to be meeting up with Big Mike. My feelings toward him were confused, at best. He was really a flirt, and I knew that was all it was, but he was also a good friend.

I crossed the border into Ecuador and slept in the same hotel in Machala that Ellen and I had found when we passed through the first time, complete with good chow mein at the *chifa*, the word for Chinese restaurants. But I scurried back to my room around 6:00 p.m., tired of being followed by snakes and other assorted Latin men. The next day, after a fruitless attempt to hitchhike, I ended up riding the bus to Cuenca.

Cuenca is a beautiful old town in a valley surrounded by mountains and gorgeous countryside of rolling hills, small rivers and eucalyptus trees. The city has colonial houses with tile roofs and cobblestone streets. It was so pretty and mellow, a smile was on my lips just to be there and not in dry, barren Peru. I glided through this beauty well into evening and arrived in Ambato at 2:00 a.m. after being hassled by the man in the seat next to me, who put his hand down my shirt every time I dozed off.

I could manage travelling alone, and at times it was fun and exciting. I always met people and was more open to adventure. But the drawbacks of being a woman alone down there were too heavy. It gave the men license to act in incredibly nervy, off-the-wall ways. I was alone for one reason only in their minds, and I could not sit in a bus or a café or walk the streets without the harassment.

Finally, I got to Baños and found a nice single room with a big bed and a wooden glassless window opening up to a view of the waterfalls at the Cordillera. Mike was around, I heard from some gringos at the café, but we had not bumped into each other yet. When we did a few days later, he said he'd heard of a cool cheap beach town on the north coast.

"Want to go?" he asked. "I wouldn't mind a few days on the beach before heading back to Colorado."

"Sounds great. Let's do it."

We had to go back to Quito to do some business and so Mike could get his plane ticket figured out before heading to the coast. He planned on going home from Quito after our trip to the beach. Short of funds, we mailed his friend in Colorado an ounce of pure cocaine, flattened into a 3-D Easter card, with the coke taped underneath a picture of Jesus, whose head moved up and down when the card moved. It was the best idea we had for how to do this, but both of us had our doubts.

If it went through and his friend sold it, we would make a few hundred bucks each. I had received a letter from my mother who said if I wanted to stay longer, she would send me money, but I wanted to avoid that and live as cheaply as possible until I got home.

It was nice to be back in Quito, a place I knew. I saw some friends and said hello to the Hotel Gran Casino. It was fun being with Mike; we did not sleep together but it was very comfortable. I wanted to wait around in Quito after Mike left, hopefully to meet up with Tom and Marcel, friends from La Paz, and travel around Colombia with them before flying home, but it was raining like crazy, as it had been every day in Quito, and I was sick of it.

"Let's split to the coast to bag some rays," I said to Mike after we mailed our Easter card. We headed to Esmeraldas, the city on the north coast, close to the border with Colombia, before catching a bus to a little beach village named Atacames.

CHAPTER 24:

ATACAMES

We spent two weeks at Atacames, my mad crush on Mike fading as I realized he was in love with Francesca, the French woman he'd met in La Paz. She'd gone back to Paris, and he was planning on flying there soon. My desire for him left, which made it all very relaxed and warm, and we were good friends.

Atacames, a tropical beach town on the north coast of Ecuador, twenty kilometers south of Esmeraldas, sat at a place where a small river fed into the ocean. It was situated on one side of the river, with a footbridge to the beach. The town was, in one word, funky. The houses were made of *guadua*, a form of bamboo, and painted bright blues and pinks, with corrugated tin roofs and wooden plank floors, complete with little geckos that lived in the bamboo slats and ate mosquito eggs. The houses provided a thin shelter against a mild climate, but the rain was hard and warped the bamboo, making the houses sink in the mud and look a little droopy. The beauty of these houses showed up from the inside, when the sunlight filtered through the slats in the daytime and the breeze came through at night.

There was a medical clinic and a church near the river, a short walk to the main square, the plaza. The plaza was bare except for a few small trees, a swing and jungle bars for a playground, next to a concrete building that housed the police station, jail, post office and municipal government, the entire bureaucracy of Atacames.

Along the beach there was a row of three or four small open-air comedors with thatched roofs and a few tables. During the week, the local families ate there, but on the weekends and holidays, the comedors served the tourists. There were a few houses farther up the beach, vacation homes for the rich, mostly empty.

The water was perfect, the sun hot, and it rarely rained that month. We stayed through Easter, witnessed a succession of gringos come and go, made friends with some of the locals, and learned the ins and outs of the coco bread bakery, the Jugo Man — who made licuados, like smoothies, out of his house on the plaza — and which restaurant had the best shrimp. During Easter week the place looked like Southern California's Balboa Island, with hundreds of tents and cars and people. Easter Break, Ecuadorian style.

We slept on the porch of a traveler house, swarming with mosquitoes, for three days, having been kicked out of our dollar-a-night hotel room to make way for the higher-paying people from Quito. There were a bunch of Brazilians there, plus assorted Europeans and some Canadians that made for a very interesting culture zap. Celos, the Brazilian, brought an Otavalan girl for her first beach experience. There she was in full traditional get-up — deep blue poncho, crisp white lace blouse and layers of skirts — walking on the beach for the first time. Her face was a mixture of curiosity and timidity as she slowly let the tide roll over her bare feet. She was quite the contrast with the locals and the tourists dressed in shorts, t-shirts and bathing suits.

A band from Esmeraldas played tropical music for three nights, and Mike and I befriended them, especially Enrique, the metal drum player. He was a very cool guy, and I intended to look him up if I ever returned. We got back to Quito to hail and thunder and too much rain. Mike decided to leave for the States after he called his friend in Colorado.

"He told me he snorted up all the coke instead of selling it. It was just too good."

"Damn, I was hoping to get that cash. Oh well. At least he didn't get busted."

I was not ready to leave and still had some money, so I booked a huge room at the Minerva hotel, a step up from the Hotel Gran Casino. After seeing Mike off to the airport, I sat alone in a café in the Indian section, drinking lukewarm black coffee, a hard tasteless roll untouched beside my cup.

"What do I do now?" I wondered, half aloud. "It's too cold here. I don't want to go home yet, but I'm too tired to keep traveling."

It had been several months since Ellen and I left California, and the journey had been so much more amazing than I ever imagined. It did not matter that we never got to Tierra del Fuego; the distances were far greater than we realized. We had traveled almost five thousand miles to get to La Paz, and then it took another two thousand miles to get back to Quito. I wasn't ready to go home yet, even though our original plan was for only six months. Besides, I still did not know what I was going to go back to: law school or work, Los Angeles or Berkeley?

I can't stay here, though, I'll freeze to death, I argued with myself silently. *I could go back to Baños. The pensión overlooking the waterfall is clean and cheap. But it's cold there, too. Maybe I'll go back to the beach. A few weeks in the sun will be great, and it's an easy place to wait for Tom and Marcel. I hope they show up soon. I'm not looking forward to a solo journey into the wilds of Colombia.*

On the way back to the hotel I was accosted by some local Mestizo men, not an unusual occurrence. But that day I was in a bad mood, and when one of the men grabbed my butt, I hauled off and kicked him in the groin with my best karate side kick, the one I remembered from my women's self-defense classes. The other men laughed.

"*Ay, la gringita está enojada!*" one man said in a taunting tone.

You bet I was angry. I stomped off quickly before they could see my tears and went to the hotel.

The following week, I ran out of Quito like a bat out of hell, having spent three days sick and miserable with fever, swollen glands, and intense fatigue. My dysentery had subsided for a while at least, thankfully. If I had been well, the social life was present and active down in Avenida Amazonas. But I split on a whim for the coast, with a night in Esmeraldas, and hurried back to the beach, where I found Tom and Marcel drinking cervezas at the Hotel Tahiti.

When Tom and Marcel decided to head up to Colombia, something about Atacames made me decide to stay. The living was easy and cheap, the beach glorious, the tropical air soft and soothing. I could feel my entire body exhale. I stayed with a bunch of hippie travelers cramped in a big open house on stilts on the north end of the beach, hidden in the palm groves. Paula, a Chilean woman with three children, was renting the house. She took me in and gave me space on the upper floor to sleep and store my pack.

Paula was tall and beautiful, with thick curly brown hair pulled back by an ivory clasp, graceful in long gauze skirts, her copper bracelets jangling as she moved. She carried a small monkey around on her shoulder and was quite the bohemian, eating psilocybin mushrooms and smoking punto rojo, a really strong weed, with Paulita and Alexandra, her teenage daughters. I loved hanging out with them and her five-year-old son Sebastian, who reminded me of Justin, my nephew, only a lot less of a brat.

The house was occupied by various other characters, as well. One was a middle-aged Brit nicknamed Jethro Tull, who wore his long gray hair in a ponytail. There were also Chilean and Argentinian émigrés, musicians, students and poets. The Chileans were there to escape the repression following the 1973 coup and assassination of Salvador Allende; the Argentines were on the run from the political violence of the Dirty War. They all sought refuge on the beach in Ecuador, where visas were easy to obtain.

I was not aware at the time of everything that was happening in their countries. My Spanish was too rudimentary to engage in real political discourse, but I understood enough to know what dangers they were escaping from. My reasons for traveling were not as serious as theirs. I was on an open-ended jaunt into interesting places, something to do because I was not ready to figure out my life. I was not a refugee but wanted to be more than a tourist. I described myself as a hippie vagabond on the Gringo Trail, a seeker of adventure and discovery, not traveling to escape anything except the high expectations of my parents and my upbringing.

I felt happier than I had been in a long time, spending time with interesting and creative people. It was definitely the right thing to do, to split up from Ellen and Sara and travel on my own. Here I could swim every day in the warm ocean, lie in the intense sun, and eat very little because of the heat. Healthy food was all around, from fresh-caught shrimp and fish to *jugos* — juices made of mango and papaya — so much better than the heavy beans and corn of the highlands. My cold went away, and I caught up on much needed rest.

Enrique and his band were coming in a few days. Life was good and full of possibilities. I decided to just hang out until it felt like the right time to leave.

CHAPTER 25:

MILICHO

The first time I saw Milicho was in a tent on the beach. He sat cross-legged on the ground and stared at me while his hands rolled weed into a joint for me to try before I bought it. I don't remember how long it was before I saw him again, but when I did, I thought the same thing I did that first day in the tent: *He is the most beautiful boy I have ever seen.*

I found myself wandering up the beach whenever Milicho and the other young men played football at low tide. I sat sometimes on the sand near where they played, giving a quick wave when he looked at me. I loved the look of his legs, the grace of his body, his perfectly sculpted arm muscles, his wide chest, narrow waist and muscular thighs. He looked so unnatural in his cheap polyester pants and multicolored patterned shirts. He was meant to be naked, a native in the wild.

Milicho was not tall, perhaps 5'5, but perfect for my 5'2. He looked more Indian than African, with chocolate-colored skin, straight black hair, high cheekbones, and a long straight nose that set him apart from the other young men there who had the curly hair and flat noses more typical of their African heritage. His real name was Rene, and no one ever told me where his nickname came from. I called him Manicho in jest, which was the name of a local chocolate candy bar, but I called him Rene in my diaries and my private thoughts of love.

One day after seeing him on the beach and saying a few words of greeting, he came over and sat down next to me on the sand. I could feel the skin on my arm tingle as he brushed up against me; my face flushed, and my breath stopped. I wanted to touch him; I wanted to feel his arms around me. My Spanish was still so basic, it is a wonder we communicated at all, but we did communicate, simply and easily.

He said, "Let us be better friends, *mejores amigos*."

"What do you mean?" I could feel the excitement in my body already building. He looked at me and smiled. "*Tu sabes.* You know what I mean."

We took a walk down the beach, to the end near the riverbank, me nervously making my best effort to chat in my halting Spanish. He was twenty, I was twenty-four. He spoke only Spanish. We went swimming, kissed in the water, then went to a secluded spot. We made love in the sand on the side of the riverbank, the sand matting my hair and scratching my bare back. Nothing needed to be said, in English or Spanish. It was done and by morning there was no undoing it.

For the next few days, we walked the beach together, and in the evenings, we made love in the sand, with the mosquitoes and the moon.

**

"*Vamos a bailar,*" Milicho said one day. He wanted to take me to the "salon" to dance.

The salon was the bar off the plaza where the locals went on Saturday nights. It was a large, bare room with wood tables and chairs along the sides, a wood slat floor slick from years of dancing, and walls reeking of tobacco and sweat. There was a bar counter in the back and a big boom box with scratchy speakers playing cassette tapes of Colombian *salsa*, Ecuadorian *cumbia*, and traditional *boleros*. Men and women drank *aguardiente*, cheap unrefined rum, and warm Coke. They danced late into the night, and drunken men wept when romantic boleros played, their heads lying on the wooden tables.

Gringos did not go to the salon. I only went across the footbridge into town to get supplies and food, otherwise I stayed on the beach with Paula and the other *extranjeros*, the travelers. But then I met Milicho, and we fell in love. And he was coming to take me dancing.

No boy had ever looked at me so directly. They usually paid little attention, had sex with me with their socks still on and the motor running. But when Milicho looked straight at me, something broke open inside me and glistened all around my heart. It was happening. He was coming for me, to choose me, to bring me into his life. All I wanted to do was fold myself into him and drown.

"You must wear a skirt and a necklace. This is a special night," Paula said as she reached into her duffle bag filled with colorful fabrics and beads to dress me up for my date.

"*Gracias por su ayuda.* I definitely need help!" I only had one skirt to wear, one that I patched together with pieces of my jeans that had fallen apart months ago. The only color I had was the red camping bandana I wore around my neck to catch my sweat. My hair — dark, frizzy brown, down to my shoulders and uncut for months — needed conditioner badly. Even my thick, wire-rimmed John Lennon glasses were scratched from months on the road. I was a mess, and now Milicho was coming to take me to the salon.

Paula garnished me with strings of puka shells, pulled my thick hair back with a ribbon, and fastened a hibiscus above my ear. She dressed me in a skirt that swayed in the breeze, while her pet monkey sitting on her shoulder clapped with approval.

"*Bueno. Ya lista,* now you are ready," she said. "Your Milicho is coming to take you dancing!"

I feel ridiculous in this skirt, a gringa hippie all dressed up like for the Renaissance Faire. What the hell, I'm conspicuous no matter what I do. I talked to myself a lot, having constant internal conversations in English.

I stood on the porch watching Milicho walk up the beach. He wore brown polyester slacks with the cuffs cut off, his sandaled feet sticking out flat below. He wore his good white shirt, and a necklace made of puka shells lying creamy white against his smooth chest. His thick black hair was combed back and glistened in the evening dark. I saw him walking up from a distance, my breath stopped by his beauty and the knowledge that he was coming for me. Everyone was excited in the house; even the monkey screamed and jumped up and down as Milicho came up the steps and handed me a banana flower. I could barely touch his skin for fear of falling into it. Whatever this was, it was happening, and all I could do was surrender.

I hugged Paula, who kissed me on both cheeks, and we set off up the beach. Milicho took my hand and wordlessly, for I did not yet know enough words, we walked across the footbridge. I knew from the solid way he held my hand and the true manner of his kiss that he was asking me to come to him, to leave the house of hippie travelers, leave the safe harbor of the Gringo Trail and step into the life of Atacames, into his life.

At the door of the salon, I stopped for a moment, but it was too late. The salon was filled with people whose conversations paused for a moment, the dancers glancing over their shoulders. Everyone noticed me standing next to Milicho. I flushed red, not from the tropical heat but from the stares. I could feel the judgment, especially from the women. *No*, their eyes told me. The hair on my arms prickled. *No.* This was not a place for tourists, travelers, blue-eyed, white-skinned hippie girls screwing their young men on riverbanks, getting high with the boys on the beach, wearing bikini tops and swimming in the ocean during the day in front of the fishermen and the children. *No*, their faces told me. Gringas did not go into the salon, did not dance with men they were not married to, did not come into this world and make messes of things.

I knew none of that, of what would happen later, as I stood in the doorway, holding tight to Milicho's hand, too filled with the lightness and the pure joy of my first love.

My life with Milicho had begun. I stepped into the salon, left Cathy behind, and became *La Catalina.*

CHAPTER 26:

LA CASITA

A few days after Milicho took me to the salon, all the travelers were kicked out of the house on the beach. Milicho and I went to see *la casita* for the first time, a one-room house in town once used by Milicho's family. When I first saw it, I thought I could never live in a place like that, so small, so run down. But the floor was good, the roof was solid, and there was a small yard lined with *chirimoya* bushes.

Milicho and I crossed over the footbridge from the beach to town, into the one-room casita. He swept the sand and dirt out the door and we stepped across the threshold. No, he did not carry me over it; we did not jump the broom or smash a glass. We did not have a wedding, but I was *casada* in the eyes of the village. "Casada," the word for married, means making a home, and that is what we did.

Our casita was made of guadua bamboo, with glassless windows with wooden shutters to close in the evenings when the mosquitoes tried to enter, following the scent of our sweat. In the mornings we made love, then opened the shutters to let in the breeze, fanned away the mosquitoes, and faced the soft, tropical morning light. There was little furniture in our casita, a thick woven mat on the floor, a table and wooden chairs, and no kitchen. We made bowls out of coconut shells and picked chirimoyas from the bushes outside the door. Chirimoyas have green, pockmarked skin, ugly like leprosy on the outside with delicious mushy pulp inside. The aroma of the blossoms filled the casita in the mornings.

I don't remember those first months; it is a dreamlike haze of time passing. I do remember our daily life. We would wake at dawn or a little later, when the chickens would come scratching and the airplane bees would buzz. Maybe we would make love on the mats. We swept out the cockroaches, greeted the scurrying geckos, and started our day. Some days it was raining too hard to go out and so we stayed inside stringing puka shell necklaces at the table, or smoking joints next to the window where the blossoms in the garden masked the smoke of pot.

Milicho always wanted to make something, to be busy with something, cooking or fishing or making necklaces to sell. And we would talk. He would tell me about his childhood, of Atacames, of his father and mother. Milicho was a bit of a star in Atacames, the goalie for the local soccer team, and the best cook in the village. No one could make *arroz con camarones* like he could. He dreamed of sailing on cruise ships, cooking for his passage. He thought about signing up for the merchant marines, or even the French Foreign Legion, seeing the world, then coming back to Atacames to open a restaurant. He had big dreams but meanwhile made money selling marijuana to the gringos who passed through and selling puka shell necklaces he made to the tourists on the beach.

Milicho told me one time, "*America debe de ser un país increíble.*" It must be an incredible place, where people talk about anything without getting in trouble. "*Aquí, no.*" Here you lay low so the army could not find you.

Here the longhair boys like him kept their mouths shut. But he didn't want to end up like his father or his older brother, drunk and old before their time, working forever in the banana plantations, drinking more when the banana fields went bust from infestation. Milicho was going to get out, go to Quito or Bogotá or even America. I would answer his questions about the States, about Los Angeles, about my family. He would sing snatches of songs, drumming on the table: "*Yo no puedo quemar, porque estoy hecho de fuego.*" I cannot burn because I am made of fire.

And we made love, a lot. Right after sunset was the best time, when it had cooled off and the mosquitoes had gone. I found the joy of making love to someone so attractive, so soft, and so loving, and Milicho was open and willing to learn.

"*Enséñame lo que sabes.*" Teach me what you know, he said, and I did, not that I knew that much. There were many good times on the mats, but many times I was uncomfortable, times he could be too rough, and too quick.

"*A veces no te toma tiempo.*" Sometimes you seem so insensitive and do not take time, I said, trying to explain my discomfort one evening after we had sex. My lack of fluency made it difficult. How could I be subtle and tactful in a language I barely had control of? But Milicho wanted so much sex, I could not keep up with him.

"*Esperate por un rato. No tengo interés ahora.*" I tried to explain I wasn't feeling horny and needed to wait, but my stumblings against the language barrier made him think I did not want him at all.

"*¿No me quieres, de repente?*" he said sharply.

"No, of course I love you, *te quiero, pero a veces es demasiado,* sometimes it is too much."

He got up, a hurt expression in his eyes, and left me alone. He came back later that night. I could smell liquor on his breath as he lay down beside me, wrapped his arm around my waist, and fell asleep.

Every day I could understand more and more of the conversations happening around me. I never realized how difficult that was going to be, given that no one spoke English. It was hard as shit, but it began to happen, and the town's attitude toward me opened as they became accustomed to my being there. I stopped being so nervous and self-conscious. My living with Milicho had become part of the town's *onda*, its vibe.

I knew I wanted to stay with Milicho for a while, to see out the momentum that was building. It was an incredible education, especially of the heart. "*Todo es posible si lo quieres; si no lo quieres, no es posible.*" Everything is possible if you want it; if you don't, it is not possible. I could not remember who said that to me on my journey, but I took it to heart. I put aside any thoughts of leaving for Colombia. I was having a love affair for the first time in my life, and it felt too good to leave.

One day in April, a few weeks after I moved in with Milicho, it was Clodoveo's birthday. Clodo was Chino's brother; they were Milicho's cousins and Chino was Milicho's closest friend. I napped a bit after an early morning of passionate awakening, then stood under the rain-spout during a hard rain, the closest thing to a shower I could get.

Then we went to town to prepare for Clodo's surprise party. My job was to distract, delay, and bring over the "victim" without him knowing what was up.

I did my task well and Clodo was duly surprised. The coconut cake the baker made was out-of-sight delicious, and someone passed around some very strong Colombian dope. There was going to be a dance that night in the salon with a *conjunto*, a live band. Life was good and I was having fun.

At 6:00 a.m. one beautiful morning, Milicho and I met up with Chino, Clodo, and Tarzan, their older brother, and Jade, a French woman who came to Atacames and got involved with Tarzan. They brought along two gringa tourists from California, women just like me, and we chatted away in English. I did not realize how much I missed gringa company. I couldn't stop talking, it felt so good to be fully understood. They must have thought I was a little crazy, like I was just let out of a cage.

We spent a day walking along the beach to Tanchique, a three-hour hike around five different rocky points, to their aunt's house inland from the beach. We stayed in a neat wood house with cows screaming in the night, roosters going at it, and turkeys in full regalia. We dined on dairy products galore, soup and fresh hot milk in the morning. Then a fast walk back, racing the tides, the gringas practically fainting from over-exposure. The following morning was incredible — a perfectly clear blue sky, and the sun hot and strong by 6:30. We headed for the beach to enjoy this place for another day.

I was beginning to realize that life really was very simple: Do good work and surround yourself with people you love. These things could be done anywhere, and I could have as full a life in Ecuador as I would have in California. I'd had so many thoughts about the necessity of being in the US, but now, that necessity was fading. I did not want to leave Ecuador when things were getting richer and more interesting solely because returning home seemed to be what I was supposed to do. I was curious to see what would happen should I become more intimately involved with a whole other culture, far from home, testing my ingenuity and ability. I was tired of moving around and wanted to stay for a little while longer in one place. I was also too damn tired to make a decision.

Staying with Milicho just felt right. That was as much of a decision as I could make.

CHAPTER 27:

THE PHONE CALL HOME

Mother's Day is next week. I should go up to Quito and get my mail and call my parents, I thought to myself as I swung in the hammock on the porch of the casita.

Time had expanded and slowed on this trip. I could not remember how long I had been in Atacames, and I could not remember where I'd been when I last called my parents. Lima, perhaps. I had done nothing for months to figure out my money plans. I loved Milicho and I wanted to be with him, and I was in no rush to get away from Atacames. But I needed to call my parents. I got out of the hammock and headed across the bridge to get ready to go.

I took the bus from Atacames to Esmeraldas, the closest town. The bus was open aired, with benches and slats above for the chickens, bananas, and bags of mail. I leaned out of the side to inhale the sweet, warm, damp, mango-scented air. It drenched me with calm and pleasure, so different from the cold highlands of Peru and La Paz where I could not catch my breath and my bones stayed chilled no matter how many layers of clothes I wore.

The bus to Quito looked like an old school bus with dirty, single-hung metal-framed windows stuck open or stuck closed, and seats torn and lumpy. I squeezed next to an Indian woman returning to the highlands, dressed in a heavy wool poncho and wide skirts. I wondered what she was doing on the coast, so out of place in a region of Black Africans. She smelled so different from them. The Indians of the highlands — the Serranos — had an aroma of mountain farms, vats of corn *masa,* and burned kindling. The Costeños — the people of the coast — did not eat corn, only rice, fish and plátanos, and their skin was scented with banana flowers and sea salt.

I settled in for the eight-hour drive up the highway to Quito, from sea level to 9,500 feet. The bus groaned loudly and lurched as the driver kept downshifting to get it up the incline, making sleep impossible. We passed through a middle temperature zone, just mild enough to grow green leafy vegetables and cucumbers, but not a single refrigerated truck existed in the area, and probably in all of Ecuador, to transport produce to the coast, where onions, tomatoes and peppers were the only fresh vegetables around.

The bus stopped at a town called Santo Domingo de Los Colorados, where the native people's faces and bodies were dyed red all over with grease mixed with *achiote*, a seed believed to have prevented smallpox. At the open market, vendors tossed vegetables wrapped in newspaper through the open windows of the bus as the riders handed them *sucres,* the money of Ecuador, in return.

The bus climbed throughout the evening and arrived in Quito just before dark. I pulled my wool poncho from my pack, put on socks and boots, and dragged my pack up to the Hotel Gran Casino, where I locked myself in my room for sleep. The next day at the embassy, the Marine behind the desk glanced at my passport and gave me some letters that were several weeks old. There was a postcard from Ellen and Sara to the embassy instructing them to hold all their mail. I assumed that meant they would be coming to Quito soon and I wondered what adventures they had been up to.

The next day I went to the telephone house, the only place that had public phones. There were private glass booths, and folding chairs in the waiting room filled with mostly Indian women, their skirts enveloping the folding chairs, their babies nursing underneath the woven layers of wool. I was the only gringo there. I put in my request for a call and settled in for a long wait.

If my folks only knew what a schlep it is to get to make a call... They better be home, I thought as I dozed in the chair. My mother traveled a lot, each year taking cash she made from her Christmas costume-jewelry business to go to Italy, France, Egypt, and Mexico. She loved travel and wanted me to have adventures, to go to exciting, life-changing places.

She took me to Europe for five weeks during my freshman year of high school, and she went to Cuba and even to China in 1978, one of the first American tourists to do so. She traveled with friends, but never with my father, not since the six months our family spent in Europe in 1955 before moving from New York to LA.

After that trip, my father never went back to Europe. He volunteered for the Israeli army for a month one time, digging latrines in the desert. After that he spent time in Palm Springs, where he did real estate investments and brought home grapefruits and cotton plants stuffed in the glove compartment of his car. Many years later, when he was living in Scottsdale, Arizona, and the temperature was 120 degrees in the shade, I asked him how he could stand to be in such heat, and why he loved being in the desert all the time.

"I spent fifty-seven days in a foxhole in the snow in the Belgian forest, and ever since then I can't get warm enough."

That was the most he ever said about the war. He was severely injured by a landmine when he was twenty-four years old, after fighting in the Battle of the Bulge in 1944, surviving by sheer luck and ending up with one leg four inches shorter than the other and his body filled with shrapnel. But in 1975, when I was on the Gringo Trail, he was happy to swim in the pool in the backyard when he was home, which was not that often. He was a lawyer, corporate CEO, and real estate investor and loved to work. He had an apartment in downtown LA, a weekend home in the desert, and came home less and less as the years passed. But that day, the day I called, he was home by the pool.

"*¡Llamada a California!* Call to California!" the man at the desk called out. I was practically asleep in the chair when the women near me began excitedly patting me on the arms, saying "*¡Llamada a California! ¡Llamada a California!*"

They are more excited than I am, I thought as I gathered my pack and entered the booth. A long-distance international call was quite the event.

The operator put the call through.

"Hello?"

"Hi Mom! Happy Mother's Day!" I said as soon as I heard her voice.

"Where the hell have you been, for Crissake?!" my father yelled from the other phone receiver. He was angry, my mother was crying. I thought someone had died. I can't remember if my mother said anything. She was not weepy by nature. In fact, she rarely cried and was hardly timid.

"Is everything ok? Are you alright?"

"Us?" he yelled. "We thought you were dead! We've been trying to find you for months. I was planning on flying to Bogotá next week!"

Apparently, my father had contacted the State Department and Henry Kissinger, someone he hated with all his soul and all his might, to get help finding me. I knew then that he was serious.

"They have a bulletin out down there to find you. Why haven't you called?"

I hadn't spoken yet. I thought about saying, I *am* calling, but I was too much in shock to be cute. My parents did not scream that often; they kept things in a bit too much, really. My mother used quiet looks of disapproval and harsh words like royal demands. My father used sarcasm, sardonic knife-sharp zingers filled with condescension and judgment, or low-pitched spits of "goddammits" and "sonofabitches," but he rarely yelled.

But boy, he was yelling now. It brought me back to their reality, out of my reverie, my pot-infused, languid chatter, the personal movie I had been in for the last few months, playing the lead and narrator simultaneously and commenting on my escapades from my mental press box. This was the consequence of too much traveling alone and too few conversations in English. I had finally found a place where I wanted to stay. I had fallen in love with Atacames, with the palm trees on the beach, the fragrance of the tropics, the softness of life. I had fallen in love with Milicho and before I realized it, months had gone by while I was through the looking glass.

"Wow, sorry. I didn't realize. I had no idea it was that long. I guess you didn't get my letters?" I lied, since I could not remember when I last wrote to them. I tried to explain what it took to make a call, but I realized they would not understand, or they had forgotten what it was like on the Mediterranean coast of Spain in 1955, where we'd lived for three months in a house on the beach in Benidorm, then a quiet, undeveloped fishing village. We had the only car, there was only electricity at night, and my father often joked that we were probably the first Jews in residence since the Inquisition. It was an experience a lot like the one I was living in Atacames.

When I made that call home, I was almost twenty-five years old. When my parents were twenty-five, it was 1945 and my badly injured father had just returned from the war to an infant son, no money, and great ambition. My mother had worked since she was fifteen and survived the war at home with her own businesses and a baby born before she wanted. My eldest brother, conceived before my father shipped out to Europe, was born in December of 1944 while my father was fighting in Belgium. By the time my parents were twenty-five, what they had learned about the world — its abject evil and unspeakable trauma, its possibilities for goodness and success, the power of hard work, family and friendship — determined who they were for the rest of their lives.

I loved them for not getting in my way, not stopping me no matter how dangerous they thought it was or how dangerous it actually was. I loved them for not insisting I come home and do something sensible. They knew I had to play out whatever it was I was doing. Besides, my older brother Richard had decided to become an actor, not the most secure of professions, and they were supportive of that. Perhaps they knew I would be safe, that my smarter, wiser, observing self would watch out for my naïve, oblivious, idiot self. So what if I wanted to hitchhike down the Pan-American Highway? So what if I wanted to live with a local boy on a tropical beach instead of going to law school? Compared to what they had experienced, my life was a jaunt, and they wanted me to get the most out of it. They just wanted me to call them now and then, so they knew I hadn't been killed in a coup or kidnapped down the Amazon.

The next day I went back to the embassy to tell them I was not lost. There was a woman behind the counter this time. When I explained why I was there and showed her my passport, she looked down on her desk and showed me a flyer that was right there, a flyer with my photo and my name and in big letters: *Have You Seen This Young Woman? If So, Contact The Embassy Immediately!*

"Who did you speak to?" she asked when I told her I came in the day before to get my mail and no one had noticed the flyer.

"There was a Marine behind the counter."

"A Marine? Oh, don't ever talk to them. They don't know anything."

We both had a big laugh at that one. I assured her I was not lost and had contacted my parents, and all was well. I picked up my backpack and headed back down to Atacames and Milicho.

CHAPTER 28:

MAGIC BUS TO THE COAST

I loved the bus ride barreling down the steep winding road from Quito to the tropical coast. It was an eight-hour ride up but only a four-hour ride down that big mountain. When we got to Santo Domingo de Los Colorados, everyone on the bus loaded up their baskets and I loaded up my backpack with perishable greens bought from the vendors, and then we headed down to the coast. It happened every time: The bus suddenly got a lot livelier as soon as we passed Santa Domingo.

The *campo*, the countryside, around Santa Domingo was solid with trees of all kinds and huge ferns because of the constant rain. As the land flattened out toward the coast, the forests had been cleared and filled with plantations of banana, cacao and coffee. The roads were unpaved dirt with farmhouses here and there, an occasional clearing with a schoolhouse, and a small tienda in someone's home. There were cows scattered around, Brahman breed, white with long horns, and groves of guava and papaya trees near small creeks.

The bus arrived in Esmeraldas, and I boarded the local open-air bus back to Atacames, everyone cheerful and light, the weight of wool ponchos lifted up and blown away by the warm breezes. The air was filled with pungent, gray heat. I sat on the bench and stuck my head into the soft warm breeze and watched the banana trees go by, one after another, grove after grove, bananas hanging heavy and green, with tails hanging down from the bunch. They had bright, upside-down red cones at the tips, ready to burst open into gorgeous, bright flowers.

Alongside the road, people in wide-brimmed straw hats and kerchiefs walked in sandals. They carried bundles of laundry or wood sticks for the stove or food from the store on their heads. Sometimes a truck passed us on the road, kicking up dust, with a bunch of men sitting on top, machetes hanging by their sides, their banana loads underneath them. Boys as young as five returning from the fields rode bareback on horses, swinging machetes.

Everything in this place was slightly damp; it had just rained and would again soon. No one thought to care or cover up; the rain was warm and friendly, plus it came and went all the time. Sometimes the air was so deeply hot and intense the rain was the only relief. The sky was usually covered with a thin gray matte finish holding in the moisture and the heat.

When I first got there, I'd longed for the cloud cover to disappear and for the sun to come out. Then it did, in a bright blue cloudless sky, burning hot and crystal clear, the yellows and blues and plant greens amplified to a new intensity. When that happened, I was excited at first. I wanted to go outside, take off my shirt, and lie in the sand and brown my skin. I stuck my arms out, turned my head up, bared my shoulders and my back to the sun. But in that one moment, I was stopped dead, my skin seared, my lungs barely able to breathe. The sun was so close, so strong, so hot, I begged for relief, for the sun to go back behind a cloud. Of course, everyone else just stayed in the shade. They thought I was nuts, like any mad dog, Englishman or hippie gringo from California who thought they knew what heat was. I was accustomed to dry heat, desert heat, mid-globe 80-degree heat, survivable heat. But in Atacames, I could get second degree burns on my feet if I walked along the beach barefoot. In Ecuador, the sun could kill. It didn't fool around.

But then there was the fruit: cherimoyas, *guanabanas* and guavas, papayas, and of course mangos, that hung in abundance in the massive trees. When the mangos were ripe, the bus driver stopped under the trees and the boys climbed up on the roof and pulled the fruit off, tossing them down to the passengers. My favorite, though, were the papaya trees, which looked a lot like Dr. Seuss creations. The trunks had no branches until an umbrella of leaves sprouted from the top of the trunk like funny hair. The papayas drooped down in green clusters like teardrops from a green cartoon giant. Goofy trees, not at all like the elegant coconut palms or graceful bananas. When the coconuts were big and green they were called *pipas*. The boys cut the tops with machetes, sliced a hole in the top, stuck a straw inside, and for a sucre they gave it to you. It was a cool drink of water with a slight taste of coconut and a tiny hint of sweetness.

The first time I picked an apple off a tree — real living, growing apples — in Oregon, I remember my excitement and the crisp sweetness of the fresh-picked fruit. I remember thinking those Pacific Northwesterners had never seen lemons and oranges grow like they did in Southern California, along sidewalks and in urban backyards.

In the upside-down perspective of the globe, southern Chile was the Washington State of South America and apples were trucked up the highway instead of down and cost five times as much as a mango. An ancient-skinned woman handed me an apple she took from a pile stacked in a pyramid on her woven blanket at the outside market, and I was grateful for a bite of that apple from the southern hemisphere, even though it was small, mealy and blotchy red. It was not delicious or crisp, but close enough to an apple for my memory to fill in the rest.

On the coast, however, everywhere I looked there was some kind of wonderfully sweet tropical fruit for the taking.

CHAPTER 29:

LIFE IN ATACAMES

Atacames appeared so idyllic, a sleepy village that had not changed for centuries — or so it seemed to me at first. The longer I lived there, I learned this was not at all true. There was very little permanence there; in fact, the place was in a state of constant change or risk of change. Nature was in charge and Atacames was at the mercy of the powers of the ocean, the rain and the earthquakes. There was a reason most people lived on the other side of the river from the beach. One day when I was walking along the beach with Milicho, I came across concrete pilings in the sand at low tide, at the north end of the beach, and asked him about it.

"*Hace mucho tiempo*," Milicho said, "*había un gran hotel.*" He told me there had been a big resort hotel here on the beach.

"*¿Qué pasó?*" What happened to it, I asked.

"*Oh, las olas se lo llevaron.*" The waves took it, he said, quite matter-of-factly. Everything except the pilings, he explained. They should never have built it so close to the water. They never came back to rebuild.

The people of the north coast of Ecuador, Costeños, were descended from Africans who arrived in slave ships and merged with the coastal indigenous people. Some enslaved people escaped into the mountains and created clandestine communities where their African dress, language, food, hair and skin survived. I remember the day some African villagers came down from the mountain for a visit to the ocean, many for the first time. I sat at a beach comedor and watched stately tall, dark women wrapped in bright African print fabric, their hair in extraordinary structures on their heads, walking slowly barefoot down the beach, holding hands, the ocean water splashing their ankles. They emerged from the mountains as if from Africa itself, intact.

The Costeño people were Black but in various shades from bitter-sweet to milk. Some men were dark-skinned and looked like they came "straight outta Compton;" others, like Milicho, looked Indian with straight noses and straight black hair. African sensibilities and stories were everywhere. People believed in *Mal Ojo*, evil eye. Señora Inez, Milicho's mother, was a *curandera*, a medicine woman, who practiced rituals similar to Candomblé, the spiritual practice in parts of West Africa that was transported to the Americas aboard the slave ships. It survived by hiding underneath the trappings of Catholicism; their ancient spirits, called *Orixás*, masquerading as saints.

There were other superstitions and visions, like *El Duende*, a phantom who wore a sombrero and got into machete fights with local men at night. As legend had it, once El Duende, who symbolized death, came into the house of Magu, a local fisherman, and tried to pull Magu's younger brother out of the bed, but Magu pulled him back. Then there was *La Pepona*, a pregnant woman who came at night and was said to eat babies. She was sometimes seen hanging around houses waiting to catch little children.

In Atacames there were children everywhere, yet the death of a child was too common an occurrence. During the winter I spent in Atacames, seven infants died of tetanus of the umbilical cord. The large extended families had lots of children to compensate for the high infant mortality rate and children were always out on the street, playing in the evenings at the plaza, running errands or hauling stuff in the mornings before school or in the afternoons. Kids were always peering into the salon, singing and dancing and roughhousing in the street. Every age had its own group, but the big kids watched out for the little kids, and everyone took care of the babies.

The children in Atacames went to school, as did Milicho, his siblings and the other cousins, but only through sixth grade. There was no high school in the village or anywhere nearby; the closest was in Esmeraldas, an hour away. There were no books in the village, only a few novellas in comic book format with single-sentence captions. There were no TVs, but there were old radios with broken antennas blaring scratchy salsa, cumbia and *wawanco* music and shouting unintelligible news reports.

People in Atacames did not analyze or reflect or discuss world events, and no one traveled outside the boundaries of their small world. There was no angst, neurosis or therapy. No one worried about what they were going to do in their lives or their professional prospects. No one ever asked me what I did for a living or what I aspired to be. They did, however, ask me when I was going to get pregnant, and why I wasn't already.

People lived each day, making sure they had food for that day, finding it, catching it, cooking it, feeding the children, washing clothes. It did not seem necessary to make much money to survive in Atacames. Everyone had a canoe for fishing, the shrimp boats that trawled up and down the coast always needed help, and the mangos and coconuts were free for the picking.

CHAPTER 30:

SEÑORA INEZ

Señora Inez, Milicho's mother, was probably the same age as my mother, who in 1975 was fifty-four, but Señora Inez's skin, wrinkled from the sun, made her look older than her years. She was a little wide in the hips with aging breasts that drooped down to the waistband of her house-dress. Her skin was light brown, there was no gray in her hair, and she had but a few upper teeth. Her feet were flat, toes splayed wide from wearing only cheap sandals and walking to the well or the river for so many years with a basket of laundry on her head. She bathed at the well, never naked, drawing a bucket up by the ropes and holding it over her head by her still powerful arms. She never got angry or upset but would often cluck her tongue against her toothless upper gum as a gesture of disappointment. She never seemed weary and when she went about her daily tasks, she moved with the same rhythm as the waves, the skirt of her dress swaying with the palm trees surrounding her.

I never found out much about her life, in part because of her missing teeth. They made her terribly difficult to understand. Señora Inez just was; she seemed to not have a past. Every day she rose before dawn, preparing her breakfast of baked plátanos — the unripe green plantains baked on the charcoal stove — salty *campesino* cheese that resembled feta, and sometimes an egg. She made strong black coffee from cold thick paste mixed with boiling water. She spent the days washing clothes, preparing rice, and cleaning fish while turning the plátanos on the hot red coals with her bare fingers.

When Milicho asked me to live with him, Señora Inez became my *suegra*, my mother-in-law. Funny how my mother never met her, never knew anything about her, even though they were in-laws for a while. She lived in a one-room casita made of guadua with a tin roof and a wood floor sitting on stilts a few feet above the sand. There was an open air *palapa* next to it with some tables and chairs where she fed tourists on the weekends. It was a lovely spot, a good walk up the beach, quietly nestled in the palm grove.

Señora Inez lived with her two daughters, both younger than Milicho. Mercedes, the older of the two sisters, was fat, big-breasted, loudmouthed, strong like a bull and always laughing raucously at my ineptness and ignorance, especially my inability to wash clothes in the basin correctly. The youngest sister, Narcissa, danced around on the verge of womanhood. She stayed the closest to Señora Inez and loved to twirl around the tables in the palapa, imagining herself a ballerina. She, too, constantly laughed at me. My struggle to learn to do the most basic tasks of everyday life was her constant source of amusement.

Every day I walked across the footbridge from our casita in town, picking up a few needed items from the little store on the bridge: sodas and margarine, perhaps a few eggs. I spent a good part of the day at Señora Inez's casita, cooling off in the hammock that was tied between two palm trees. When Milicho did not go off to bring in the fish net from the river, we would go to the beach together to eat breakfast with his mother and sisters and stay to help prepare the daily meal, cooking rice in a large pot turned black from the charcoal and frying fresh fish in a flat pan while the *plátanos verdes* baked on the coals.

Milicho's older brother, who was married and not as handsome as his brother, lived in town. His face was pock-marked and light skinned, not the creamy skin of his younger siblings. As far as I knew, their father was not around. I was told he and Señora Inez had divorced a long time ago and Milicho never spoke of him, but one day I asked Señora Inez about Milicho's father.

"*No vive aquí*," she said. He doesn't live around here. "*Se fue. Vive lejo*s." He is gone, lives far away. She said she hadn't seen him in twenty years.

She was not too forthcoming with additional information, so I let it go. There were a lot of things that were not talked about, a lot of questions I asked that were answered with a shrug or dismissive silence. Some things I just did not get because of the hole in my comprehension, so I let the mystery remain. Chino once mentioned that Milicho's father was a drunk, but that did not seem to be too unusual around there.

One evening, sometime after my conversation with Señora Inez about her estranged husband, I sat with Milicho in the town plaza watching little kids playing on the swings in the sandy lot. We had just sat down with our licuados from the Jugo Man, a mix of mango, banana, chirimoya and papaya, milk, and ice made in a blender that sat in an open window of his house. The air was still warm and humid, and the licuados provided some relief. An old man, one I had not seen before, came over to talk to Milicho. He was skinny and toothless, and his pants were too short above his sandaled feet. Milicho walked away from me to talk to him out of earshot. There was no expression on his face to give away any content of the conversation. When the old man finally left, Milicho sat down to finish his licuado.

"*¿Quién es?* Who was that?" I asked, as I often did.

"*Mi padre,*" he said matter-of-factly.

"What? *Tu padre?* That was your dad? But I thought he lived far away?" I asked if he had come back for a visit.

"*Hable en serio. ¿Qué estás diciendo?* What are you talking about?" he said. "He lives in town with my brother. I don't have much to say to him."

I thought about that for a long time. The walk from the casita where I lived with Milicho to Señora Inez's house on the beach took maybe twenty minutes at the usual tropical pace, strolling in sandals on the hot sand. Señora Inez never went into town. She had not crossed over a distance I walked every day, perhaps a mile, in twenty years. Years ago, her husband left her and moved far away, across the short footbridge, and they had not spoken since. In all that time, she had never crossed the bridge and neither had he. Atacames covered an area the same size as my high school and had a thousand people at most, half of them children. That was the size of their universe. There were no cars, a few bikes, some canoes, and a daily bus to Esmeraldas, as far away to Señora Inez as China or Mars, as far away as *Los Estados,* California, or Los Angeles.

One day, Señora Inez clucked her toothless gums as she watched me wash my shirt on the tin washboard at the well.

"*Ay, Catalina,*" she sighed. "*Tu no sabes nada de la vida.*"

"I do so know about life," I mumbled to myself in English. "Just not this one."

Mercedes took the washbasin next to me, hauled up a bucket of water from the well, and began to wash the shirt on the washboard, as she did every day. I never could get the hang of it, washing clothes at the well. I struggled to get all the soap out, and my clothes were stiff with salt water and leftover soap, my cut-off jean shorts hopelessly stained, my t-shirts shredded by the washboard. I remembered when Ellen and I tried unsuccessfully to wash our jeans in the river in Peru, smashing them on the rocks like the local women were doing, leaving them stiff and shredded.

When Mercedes showed me how to push on the clothes to get the soap out, her arms, big, brown and powerful, pushed the cotton piece up and down, up and down, in rhythm with the breeze, somehow magically cleaning the dirt and rinsing out the soap in one continuous movement. She stood at the wash table made of palm bark and tin, the basin lower than waist height, and grabbed piece after piece of pants, shirts, t-shirts and blouses made of poor-quality cotton, scrubbing and rinsing each item one by one. She showed no sign of fatigue, singing softly along with the waves. She hung each piece on the line strung between two palm trees, then swayed in the hammock while the clothes dried by the equatorial sun, the perfect blue water just a few feet away, the sand too hot to touch except where we stood under the palm canopy. One needed strength for this life, and patience. I had a lot to learn, as Señora Inez often told me. Washing a t-shirt at the well was the first of many lessons.

I learned to wash my hair and body at the well, too, holding a bucket of water over my head with one arm, washing with the other. I learned to use as little potable water as possible, since every drop had to be carried in buckets from the water trucks. I learned how to pee on my feet to disinfect the mosquito bites so I would not get staph infection. I was a novice in the art of basic environments, learning where the water came from, how to live without light switches and glass. I became comfortable in a life closer to the ground as my comprehension of my surroundings, of the language, slang, and nuances improved in time. I was more aware of what I did not know and did not understand the longer I was on this journey, and I lost the pretense of knowing what I was doing. I learned to ask for help, to breathe deeply to lessen the crimson showing in my cheeks, and to rely on the wisdom that was all around me.

One day I sat in the hammock and wrote a poem:

Deluged with Love

I pull the bucket up from the well in the sand in the
grove of coconut palms next to the ocean.
I pull the bucket up filled with sweet, fresh water
kissed with bits of salt and ocean fragrance.
I pull the bucket up and try to hold it over my head with one arm,
To wash my hair with the other.
But I am not yet strong enough,
Not yet knowing enough
How to live this life, this life of washing myself,
my body, my hair, from a bucket
Poured over my head from a well in the sand
nestled in the coconut palms,
The sound of the waves nearby.
I am not yet adept at living this life.
My arms are not strong enough,
My hands not calloused enough against the rope tied to the bucket.
I pull the bucket up and spill it more times try-
ing to hold it up over my head.
I try again and feel the strong hands of Mercedes,
my lover's sister, close over mine,
Gently taking the rope into her calloused hands.
I feel her powerful smooth forearms lift up the bucket,
Like lifting up a leaf.
I hear her laughter as she swings it up over my head,

Gesturing through her laughter for me to
lather myself with soap, which I do,
Ungracefully,
Shyly trying to reach the parts hidden inside my bathing suit.
Mercedes pours the sweet, cool, salty water slowly over my head, my body,
My heart.
Ay Catalina, she giggles, as she pulls up another bucket,
Another bucket for my bathing,
Another bucket filled with her love.

CHAPTER 31:

THE RHYTHM OF LIFE

I began to settle into the daily life of Atacames, a tourist town whose rhythm of activity ebbed and flowed with the holiday calendar. My life in Atacames moved with a soft tropical rhythm, the daily routines were simple and unchanging like the equatorial tides.

It hadn't always been a tourist town; the area was once filled with banana plantations, owned by a few companies, like Dole, and everyone worked planting, harvesting, and hauling bananas by river boats to the harbor, where the stalks were loaded onto ships bound for the north. Then about ten years before I arrived, a disease wiped out some of the nearby plantations and the companies pulled out for areas farther south, writing it off as a tax loss and leaving Atacames without an industry or economy.

The families had to develop businesses to cater to the tourists and students who came to the beach. Everyone worked in comedors, tiendas, or in the two hotels at the north end of the beach. There was the Jugo Man, a few tailors, a bakery, fishermen providing seafood for the comedors, washerwomen and delivery boys. Atacames was also a distribution center for the surrounding farms, a midpoint for gathering and trucking fruit, cacao, coffee, and bananas bound for Esmeraldas. The green cacao beans were spread out to dry on a huge cement square lot in the middle of town. Some men worked on the never-ending jobs of road repair and the production of charcoal, the main source of cooking fuel.

Everyone was busy helping, including the children, who were incorporated into the work of the family as soon as they could walk. In a system like this, where children are depended on and utilized in the economic well-being of the family, large families were a source of pride.

There was a real feeling of love and closeness, partly out of necessity, since the whole town was one extended family. I wanted so badly to be part of this family, this community, so far away from my own.

I was living in a poor area in one of the poorest countries in the world. In Atacames, everyone except the rich people lived in one-room houses, without toilets or running water, cars or machines, where one hundred sucres or four dollars was a lot of money. But the longer I lived there, what I saw every day became normal: I forgot that this was poverty. The quality of life was in everyone's gaiety and industry and love for each other. I forgot that my neighbor's house was poor because I was living the same way, shitting in the bushes, hauling drinking water every day, sleeping on a mat on the floor. And yet I was not suffering. That was the key word: suffering.

Here the people did not suffer like the poor in the Sierra, where the land gave them so little. On the coast the land was kinder, the climate mild, the area rich in fish and fruit, and no one starved. The warmth of the climate made for a warmth in their lives, and the poverty made the importance of love and families and children and fiestas even greater. I was learning every day that if I could be happy and lead a rich life that was materially poor, once I discovered the simplicity of life, I would never need to be dependent on wealth to bring me happiness.

Each day I discovered more about the town that I would never have known as a tourist. One day Milicho stopped at the house on our corner to buy *arroz con leche*, a delicious, sweet rice pudding.

"What?" I exclaimed. "I thought the only place to get it was at the tienda on the bridge. How did you know there would be arroz con leche here?"

"*Siempre hay allá*," he said. "There is always arroz con leche here."

How long was it until I discovered there was a second bakery at the edge of town or that Pepe Sanchez's tienda had cold Cokes? How long did it take me to figure out who was or had been married to whom, who were actual blood cousins when everyone called each other *primo*? I was invited to take a slice out of the pie that was Atacames, to taste a piece of their lives, a puzzle to put together, and the more I learned, the more complex and richer it became.

Preparing meals in Atacames started with a canoe ride at dawn out to the shrimp boats. Milicho worked on the fishing boats, hauling in the nets and bringing back buckets of mackerel and *langostinos* to fry up in Señora Inez's comedor. He gave whatever was left to the other families. Milicho took me out to the boats a few times in a canoe. He rowed us up and over the waves, standing up in the canoe like an Incan warrior, the oar like a spear in his hand, bare-chested and strong and in control of the sea. We boarded the old wooden trawler and sat in a circle on the main deck on short wooden benches, small wooden shovels in our hands as the sailors, in shorts with bare chests, their skin baked brown, their feet rough with toes splayed wide from a life without shoes, dumped the nets from the ocean onto the deck.

We sorted out the mess of ocean matter piled high in the middle of the circle, the stench of seaweed, fish and salt intense as the sun warmed our backs. I learned to recognize and fill the metal buckets with the good stuff — the shrimp, langostino, crawfish, squid and mackerel — and push the inedible nasty sea gook of Moray eel, jellyfish and ugly tentacled slimy things back into the ocean through the holes in the sides of the boat. Sometimes Milicho sent me to flirt with the captain so that he would give me a few more buckets of seafood in addition to the ones we earned by helping the crew. I wanted to sit on the deck working with the crew, but Milicho didn't like the way the men looked at me. He thought I was too curious about everything and did not like it when I talked to men I didn't know.

We loaded the buckets into the canoe, four or five buckets on a good day, and headed back to shore. Sometimes we lost a bucket or two in the breakers getting back to the beach, the shrimp and squid swimming for their lives or floating on the surface, already dead. Back on the beach, we divided up our catch with other families for their comedors, taking only what we could cook that day. There was no refrigeration, so everything had to be cooked right away or thrown out.

After breakfast I spent the next few hours cleaning shrimp and squid. I stood next to a long wooden table just out of the sun, my hands in a huge wooden bowl filled with water. After washing the shrimp a few times, I took each one, pinched off the end of the tail, broke off the heads, and slit the shell along the underbelly, removing the thin black line with my fingernail and rinsing it away into the bowl.

"That's *caca de los camarones*, shrimp poop," Milicho said. "Always take it out."

I spent hours ripping shells off shrimp bodies and cleaning out lines of poop, working faster each time. The langostino were easier to clean. I kept the shell and head on, slit the belly, removed the poop line, and dipped it into salt. The calamari were more of a challenge: blue ink spurted out when I cleaned them and got on everything. Cleaning them took forever, cutting their rubbery heads off and leaving the edible tube pieces clean. Sometimes I cleaned juvenile hammerhead sharks, cutting off their small little perfect shark faces and fangs before slicing the body down to the tail. Years later, I laughed at the irony that, while my brother Richard was shooting *Jaws* in the States, his kid sister was somewhere in the tropics, cutting off sharks' heads with a machete. I was completely unaware, living in Atacames, what a big deal that movie was or how famous my brother would become because of it. The only thing I heard was in a letter my mother sent me, which said: *Your brother is making a movie about a big fish. I think it's a mistake.*

When I finished cleaning the seafood, it was time to make the meal. I put garlic pieces under the shell and inside the slit of the langostino, which was fried whole in hot oil. The shrimp was boiled and mixed with rice, red achiote and garlic to make arroz con camarones. The achiote oil was for color; it had no discernable taste but the slight pale red tint it gave the rice made the dish taste even better somehow. Some of the shrimp we made into *ceviche*, marinating them in nothing but lime juice, garlic and cilantro. The calamari were fried in hot oil, garlic and pepper and served with the usual white rice and *minestre*, the dish of boiled kidney beans. Tomato, onion and cucumber cut up on the side made the salad.

Milicho and I spent a lot of time together, cooking meals and walking on the beach. There never existed in our relationship the traditional roles of married men and women so prevalent in the village. Milicho was different from the other men in that respect, more willing to change and grow and learn new ways. I called him a hippie, and I meant it in the best sense of the word. He was part of the counterculture, breaking away from the establishment. Yet he still had many of the ways of the Latinos deeply embedded in him and hard to get out. One day I went shell hunting with a gringo traveler friend. Milicho was so pissed at me, and jealous that I would go with another man for the day. It became a crisis of principle.

"*¿Qué pasa?* What is the matter with you?" I asked him when I got back. "*No me besaste.* You refused to kiss me when I left in the morning."

Milicho looked at me angrily. "*¿Qué estabas haciendo con ese gringo?*"

"*¡No hice nada!*" I yelled. "I didn't do anything! Chino told me you broke into tears in the salon. *¿Por qué? ¡Celoso! ¡Sin razón!* Jealous of me for no reason!"

I did not realize at the time how resentful he must have felt about all the conversations he did not understand, the time I spent with gringos instead of with him. I had a world he could not enter, and it must have hurt.

But we sure had fun. We danced and got high and laughed. We helped in Señora Inez's comedor, making jokes about the tourists, watching their faces as we walked away together, arm in arm. A few times he took me to his aunt's farm in Tonchigue and laughed at me for refusing fresh warm milk. He laughed at my mistakes in Spanish and laughed even more when I said something slang. It must have been funny to hear me be vulgar like *los muchachos.*

And he loved to speak English. He would ask me a hundred things a day. "How do you say, 'Do you like fish?' How do you say, 'I love you?'" I taught him to say, "Eat shit, motherfucker," with instructions to say that to a gringo who was insulting. And he did, quite a few times, to the utter shock of the gringos around. We spoke English a lot to each other. He would come up to me in the salon and say, "Let's go; I want to go home," and walk off feeling proud that los muchachos did not understand. Many times, I watched him run out to the surf with a big log of driftwood to save some tourists from Quito from drowning in the riptides, then call them motherfuckers in English when they left without so much as a thank you. Milicho had his pride, that's for sure. And a bit of arrogance too, like all Costeños.

CHAPTER 32:

A QUICK TRIP ACROSS THE COLOMBIAN BORDER

A few months after Milicho and I moved into the casita, I needed to go to Quito to renew my visa. We were also getting low on pot, and I was getting low on cash. It did not take much to live in Atacames, a few sucres every day for groceries was sufficient, but I would need more if wanted to stay in Ecuador. I did not want to ask my parents, not until I really needed enough for the flight home. I decided to hop over the border to Colombia to buy some pot to sell back in Atacames for cash. I knew a guy in Pasto, a small city near the border, who could set up a deal.

In one night and day, I traveled from Atacames to Pasto, by bus up to Quito, then hitchhiked really fast across the border. In Pasto I did a little shopping in the center of town and found football shoes for Milicho. The next day was a cloak-and-dagger walk through Pasto with my friend, where we met up with a seller in some side alley. I scored a kilo, then my friend took me to a grove of eucalyptus by the river, surrounded by gorgeous Colombian campo. We got stoned, and when he made a pass at me, I turned him away, explaining that I was in love with someone. I really was telling the truth. I did not want anyone but Milicho, something that was new for me. It frightened me to want someone so much.

I took a bus back to the border with the kilo flattened and taped to my abdomen inside my jeans, covered by my thick wool poncho. I was pretty chunky, so it did not look weird. I checked into the small border office on the Ecuadorian side. There were a few soldiers outside, and one uniformed army officer inside the small office filled with just a desk and a few chairs. I must have been quite a sight: a solo female hippie traveler in jeans and boots and poncho, blue eyes and red bandana, just the sort of girl the men thought were fair game, *putas*, easy hippie chicks. When I gave him my passport, he looked up at me with a smirk on his face.

"*Si tu quieres tu pasaporte, tu sabes lo que quiero.*" He told me I could not get my passport back unless I fucked him. Just like that. No shame, just standard transactional behavior. I was more concerned about him grabbing me and finding the pot than I was of him, so I reached into my best Ecuadorian Spanish.

"*¡Cuidado, va a tener bastante problemas si me tocas!*" I lied about how my father worked for the embassy and said he was going to be in big trouble if he touched me. I raised my voice in outrage, dropping names of important operatives I had read about in Philip Agee's book about the CIA in Ecuador that had just been smuggled into the country. Thankfully, my decent Ecuadorian accent saved my ass.

"Ok, *pues.* Fine," he said, with a slight laugh. "*Hasta la próxima,*" as he tossed my passport at me. "Maybe next time."

It was a good thing it was so cold there, so the soldiers could not see the sweat on my forehead. I quickly got on the bus and could not stop shaking.

That was a close one, I thought as I steadied my breathing. *I must be completely crazy, or stupid, or bored.*

I had to wait a few days in Quito for my visa, and I left as soon as it was approved. All I was concerned about was getting back to Atacames as soon as possible. I was tired of the rain and the cold and exhausted from the stress of the trip. I missed Milicho and I wanted to see his face when I unzipped my pants.

**

When I got back to Atacames and walked in the door of the casita, Chino and Clodo were making necklaces and smoking a joint, so my arrival with the kilo caused no intense enthusiasm. Milicho seemed pissed at something and hardly said a word to me. I did not know why, and it was a weird welcome back. I could tell by Milicho's wide-eyed expression that he was blown away by the shoes I brought him, but instead of a thank you, I got the usual accusations of infidelity. He assumed I had been with someone on this trip.

"Milicho, *¡no es justo!* You accuse me of fucking others in Quito, which I didn't do!" It was hard enough dealing with the male sex, but it was ridiculous trying to communicate in another language. It took me several minutes and checking my dictionary to put together the sentences.

Finally, I said, "How can you throw such shit at me for things I don't do but that you only imagine, when at the same time it is you who is unfaithful?"

I tried to tell him how fucked up that kind of contradictory sexist bullshit was, hampered by my limited Spanish. I had the accent down, but complexity and nuance were still difficult.

"*¿No lo ves?* Don't you see? You slept with Gloria the *Brasiliera* when I was in Quito last time and our relationship is not destroyed. *No es destruido. Te amo todavía.* I still love you. So lay off me with your feelings of guilt."

Milicho stopped me. "*¡No, no me digas mas!* I don't want to hear about it anymore," he said and ran out.

We met on the corner, late that night. I will never forget, he looked so sad, so vulnerable. He said, "*Yo quiero cambiar.* I am trying not to be so jealous, but it takes a long time to change. *¡Por favor, perdóname!*" And I did forgive him, and I loved him even more after that.

It rained practically every day for the next few weeks. We stayed in the casita until late, rolling joints and making puka shell necklaces. One morning, Milicho and I made passionate love on the mat, my hip bones sore from being pushed too hard, then Milicho left to go to the fishing boats. It rained in full sheets of warmth and the sandy ground surrounding the casita turned to mud. I set some coconut bowls outside to fill up for a shower later, but when the rain came down harder, I put on my bathing suit and stood outside in the rain to wash off the sex, and the loneliness.

There were certain difficulties about living in a place as basic as Atacames, especially for women. I did not have a shower or toilet or running water. I had to handle my sanitation like I was tent camping in the wilderness, boiling water for cleaning and bathing, disposing of waste in safety and privacy. When I had my period, it was a challenge to keep clean, and I hoarded my supply of tampons, a luxury in this life, like precious gems. At least I didn't have to figure out how to shave my legs and underarms. Being a hippie had some advantages. I had my diaphragm for birth control, the only method I used after the IUD I'd been given after my abortion was removed. I had bled so intensely, hemorrhaging for ten days a month, before I begged to have it taken out. I found out later that the IUD I had, the Dalkon Shield, was taken off the market in the United States, only to be dumped on women in places like Ecuador.

I found out a lot of things about women in this part of the world, places poorer and less developed than the United States. I thought I knew what women wanted; I was an activist in the feminist movement and fought for abortion rights when I lived in Berkeley. When I traveled through Latin America, and especially living in Atacames, I learned that I didn't know shit about what women wanted. I was seeing the world through the lens of my arrogance and privilege. I wanted safe birth control and access to a safe abortion when I needed one. Women in places like Ecuador wanted healthy children who survived infancy, who did not succumb to tetanus of the umbilical cord or dysentery. They wanted to have as many children as possible, knowing how many would not survive into adulthood. These women did not want to be given IUDs; they wanted access to prenatal care and safe deliveries.

In Atacames I was afraid to use my diaphragm because of the difficulty of sterilizing it and keeping it from getting moldy in the tropical heat. I could not share my struggles with birth control in a place where no one else practiced it, or with a partner who would not understand or support it. Instead, I tried to absent myself when I was ovulating, something I actually could feel when it was happening. I was living in a place without electricity, so close to the earth, on the equator, where the pull of the tides and the moon are especially strong, and I would time my trips up to Quito or feign illness to avoid sex. This worked well, until one day I thought it hadn't.

"Dammit, I think I may be pregnant, no joke!" I murmured to myself one morning, realizing my period had not come that month. I had two choices: go to Guayaquil and get an abortion for forty dollars or have a baby. I was not with Milicho long enough to decide to have a child with him, even though Milicho really wanted one. If I had a child, it would bring on a monstrous change in my life; a change not altogether unwanted, but a change I'd assumed would not happen for a while. It would certainly answer the question of my staying or not. But I did not feel strong enough to do this, physically or mentally. The dysentery that still attacked me now and then weakened me, and where and how I was living was not healthy for a pregnancy or for an infant. On the other hand, if I had an abortion, I knew it would change my relationship with Milicho and with the village, possibly ending the whole thing. Abortion was not something anyone did there, ever. Either way, I was headed for a tumultuous explosion in my life.

After a week of intense imagining being pregnant and being a mom, I started to get used to the idea, finding myself a little excited, along with feeling worried and scared. I was almost twenty-four years old, an age when women did get married and have children. I knew friends from school who were already mothers.

I took a long walk down the beach to the far end away from everyone, sat down and cried out loud, "Mom, Dad, help me! I am stuck and I don't know what to do."

I prayed to my parents, as if I were waiting for an answer from the divine, but no answer came, and I left the beach just as confused as to what I should do.

Then I woke up in the morning with bloody sheets and a huge sigh of relief. That day I was in a terrific mood; I felt free again and the pressure was off. I could relax and enjoy the fun of living in Atacames, but for how long, I could not say.

CHAPTER 33:

THE COOKIE LADY

After living in Atacames for several months, one thing was clear: I needed a project, something to do. I really missed chocolate. Real chocolate. Bittersweet chocolate. Toll House cookie chocolate. In Ecuador, the best I could find was a sandy, grainy milk chocolate bar, the coarse white sugar barely blended into the bland, cheap oily chocolate. Even though Ecuador was a cacao-producing country, I blamed this sad excuse for chocolate on the evils of imperialist trade policies. All the good chocolate was exported out of the country. And forget the cookies. The South American version of a cookie was somewhere between baby teething wafers and sugary hardtack. I was dying for a good chocolate chip cookie, as if all my longing and homesickness for the States could be rolled up into my desire for one crunchy, gooey, delicious lump of America. So, one day I decided to make them myself.

"*¿Puedes conseguir chocolate? ¿Buen chocolate, en trozos?* If Ecuador produces chocolate, can I get some? Good stuff? Chips, perhaps?" I asked Milicho one day, my eyes bright with hope and desperation.

"*Seguro.* Certainly," he said. "For what?"

"Cookies," I said. "*Galletas.* We'll make them."

Frankly, I was so bored by then I was happy to create a business, an occupation, and a purpose. I had already introduced guacamole and veggie omelets and scrambled eggs and onions to the unsuspecting and much appreciative tourists at Señora Inez's comedor. But now I wanted to make real Toll House chocolate chip cookies with real good chocolate chips.

"*Bueno,*" Milicho said. "I'll see what I can find."

I wrote a friend from Berkeley and asked her to mail me the recipe for Toll House cookies that comes on the back of the chocolate chip bag. The empty bag arrived flattened in an envelope a few weeks later. Milicho and Chino built a table and packed it with sand to use as a stove. They brought over some pots and pans from the comedors, and I bought plates and mixing bowls in Esmeraldas. Milicho came back a few days later with a slab of chocolate as big as a two by four, and we were off and running.

Pablo, the baker's pothead son, said I could bake my cookies in his father's oven. The oven was a tropical version of the ovens in Bruegel's medieval urban landscapes — a big, round, clay structure, heated by coals, very deep and red hot like a giant pizza oven. Pablo and his father wore white aprons and used long wooden paddles to move the loaves of bread in and out, an unexpected scene in the middle of a beach town in the tropics. I made a deal with Pablo, trading joints for oven space, and began the search for the rest of the ingredients. Being the natural food hippie from Berkeley that I was, I wanted to make the cookies with whole wheat flour instead of the white flour called for in the recipe. The merchants thought I was crazy or mistaken in my Spanish.

"¿*Tiene harina de trigo integral?*" I asked.

"*Tu no quieres esto, tu quieres harina blanca.* You don't want that. You want white flour," they insisted.

I tried again. "*Si, yo quiero integral.*"

"*No tenemos eso, eso nos dan a los puercos.*"

No one had any; they said whole-wheat flour was fed to the pigs. I had to give up my hippie communal absolutist adherence to all things wholegrain and ordered white bleached flour in five-pound bags, white sugar in bulk, and margarine instead of butter, which was very expensive with no way to keep it cool. Milicho took a machete and chopped up the slabs of chocolate into little chunk pieces, not quite teardrop shaped chips, but passable.

I made the first batch and waited for the outcome with fervor and anticipation. I took a bite and almost broke a tooth. The taste was reminiscent of sweet cookie dough, but they came out hard as rocks. I had forgotten the baking soda. I spent the next weeks searching every market until I finally found bicarbonate, baking soda, at a pharmacy in Esmeraldas.

Finally, my career as the village *galletera*, The Cookie Lady, was born. For several weeks, I made batches of eight hundred cookies at a time, filled up a big basket, and walked from the town to the beach to sell the goodies to the tourists. The children followed me like the Pied Piper.

"*¡Galletera! ¡Galletera! ¡Dame una! ¡Regalame una!*" they yelled as I tossed the broken pieces at them. The gringo tourists on the beach haggled me about the price.

"One sucre, are you kidding? That's too much." A sucre was worth about ten cents.

"Give me a break," I snarled. "When was the last time you had a chocolate chip cookie, huh? And you are not willing to spend a dime for the real thing?"

Eventually, my business revealed itself to be unprofitable, as I ended up feeding too many cookies to my stoner friends who tossed sucres at me and ate far more than they paid for. It reminded me of my Berkeley days selling sandwiches for Moveable Feast and tossing leftovers to my roommates in exchange for quarters.

Years later, after returning from Ecuador and moving to a house in Venice Beach, a neighbor of mine was sure she had met me sometime in the past. After several conversations, we finally figured out we were in Ecuador at the same time, and they had even been to Atacames.

"Wait! You are the Cookie Lady!" she cried. "We bought chocolate chip cookies from you on the beach. I'll never forget that. They were terrific!"

My fame as La Galletera had spread across the globe.

CHAPTER 34:

ANOTHER AUGUST – 1975

August, my birthday month, arrived in Atacames, marking a year since Ellen and I started out on the Gringo Trail. My life with Milicho continued to be sweet, if not always easy. We had a little birthday celebration in the casita, with a cake that Pablo made for the occasion. Otherwise, life was uneventful, save for the three-day Fiesta de Atacames at the end of August, when all the houses blossomed into restaurants to sell *caldo de gallina* —chicken soup — and fried fish at outrageous prices to the tourists.

There were crowds of students and visitors from Quito and Cuenca, and locals from Esmeraldas. Everyone danced until dawn, then started all over again the next day. The party did not stop for three days and three nights straight and the families made the money they needed for several months. So much aguardiente and beer was consumed that the whole town seemed to stay drunk for days.

After the festival, Atacames quieted down, and the locals went back to their daily lives until the next wave of tourists descended on the beach for the Easter holiday.

Milicho and I partied a bit together during the festival, but I could not keep up. I was never a big drinker or a late nighter, and the dysentery continued to plague me. I stayed close to home, catching up with Milicho when he came back for sleep or sex. His appetite for sex was insatiable, much more than mine, and I could not keep up with that, either. One night he came in late from the festival, quite drunk, and when he lay down on the mat, he was not too tired to roll on top of me.

"*¡Ay, Milicho, es demasiado!* Too much and I can't feel. And the mats are so hard, if I am pinned to the floor, it kills my feeling." I made a pact with myself not to give in and only fuck when I felt like it. I could hear the line from the Rolling Stones in my head, "You can't always get what you want."

"It would help if we got a mattress!" I pushed him off but held him close.

"*Bueno, tu no me quieres.*" Milicho was cold to my caresses. I got really scared of losing him and cried real tears. I was silent for a moment, trying to arrange the sentences in his language, with the nuance and depth I did not yet have. I tried to tell him the truth, that I was a little scared of really jumping in, but I did love him.

"*Te quiero, por sierto.* Sometimes I don't show it. It scares me a little. *Tengo un poco miedo.*"

"*No te creo,*" he said. "You only say you love me to have sex with me."

"I know I can be distant and casual sometimes. *No puedo comunicarse bien mis sentidos,* because of the difficulties of communicating my feelings."

But I knew I did not express my emotions that well and it had nothing to do with the language barrier. I had to learn to show him I cared, despite my fears. Everyone needed a bit of passion, and he needed to see it in me. I also realized there was not much more we could share except caring deeply for each other's happiness and loving each other sexually and emotionally.

I can't worry about this stuff, I thought, after we settled into sleep. *Just stay and dig it.*

**

A few weeks later, I needed to go to Quito to renew my visa again and cross the border into Colombia to buy more weed. Milicho insisted on traveling with me.

I agreed, reluctantly. I knew this was a risky thing to do, taking Milicho with me, but he was adamant. Black Costeños were not welcome in the cold highlands. The people in Atacames wore their Blackness proudly but rarely traveled or lived away from the coast.

After the eight-hour bus trip up from the coast, we arrived in Quito. We stopped in a café to get some food before walking up the winding cobblestone streets to the Hotel Gran Casino. A Castilian man in a suit sitting at the next table leaned over to me and spoke English.

"What are you doing being with that monkey?" He gestured at Milicho and laughed. I was too shocked to respond. Milicho did not need me to translate and just glared at the man in silence.

At the Hotel Gran Casino, the young man at the reception desk was from Uruguay, with white Castilian skin and a haughty, condescending attitude.

"What is he doing here?" he said in English and motioned towards Milicho, a nasty tone in his voice.

"He's with me," I said, a bit surprised by the unfriendly greeting.

"Well, he can't stay here. And you two can't stay here together, that's for sure."

Milicho didn't say anything, but I could feel his foot start to tap nervously.

"Like hell he can't!" I said loudly. "He's staying here, and he is staying here with me!"

I was in the man's face with all the gringo sense of privilege and power I could muster, aware of Milicho's silence and muted pride. He did not understand the English words but understood all too well the man's animosity. We took our backpacks up to the room and made our plans. Milicho insisted on going to the border by himself, his macho pride now in need of satisfaction. I couldn't talk him out of it. I described the man I had met with the last time, and where it was, the plaza across from the church, in Pasto, the town across the border.

"Ask for Pedro and he'll sell you the stuff."

Milicho took the fifty US dollars — a fortune there — my sleeping bag, his jacket and pack, and left. I waited all the next day and into the next evening and still he did not come. I went down to the front desk several times and the Uruguayan insisted he had not shown up.

By nighttime I was frantic. Finally in the early morning hours, there was a knock on my door and the night reception clerk stood there with Milicho, who was dirty, shivering and empty-handed.

Milicho sat on the bed, a blanket wrapped around him; he could barely speak. He was just a boy in that moment, freezing, exhausted and scared. He'd met up with the guy named Pedro, who — rather than selling him weed — ripped him off, stealing the cash along with his jacket and sleeping bag. He hitchhiked back to Quito and got to the hotel in the evening but the *pendejo* at the front desk wouldn't let him in the hotel. Milicho spent the night outside on the street, in the cold.

"*Puta su madre, cabron!*" he spit, tears just behind his black deep eyes, his body stiff like stone. I hugged him and knew I should never have let my young, sweet boy go on such an errand.

I was exhausted, furious, fighting tears. Ecuador in the 1970s was like the United States in the 1950s, enamored with plastic Tupperware and washing machines and racist as hell. When I asked to speak to the owner to complain, the Uruguayan asshole just laughed and said, "I'm in charge here." We did not want to stay there another night and headed into the cold.

None of the pensiones in the Indian section would rent to us. The big fancy hotels in the tourist area would not let me use their toilets, let alone give the two of us a room. I did not have enough cash to stay there in any case. We were desperate to find a safe, warm place for the night. We headed down the steep narrow streets, through the widening boulevards of the commercial district and down the steep steps to the suburb of Guápalo, a tiny hamlet of old houses, a church, and a little market. We heard from some travelers at the Gran Casino about a free house run by the church that provided shelter for travelers and homeless people.

The dirt road was lined with old adobe walls of cracked plaster hiding ancient houses. There were no streetlights, and there was a slight odor of urine, roasted corn and kerosene. It was already dark when we arrived at the church, a large stone structure with cold, damp plaster walls, concrete floors and windows with cracked glass and old iron grates. There were a few large rooms, and corridors leading off them to other dark rooms and the empty chapel. Electricity was long gone; there were only candles and flashlights for light. During the day the natural equatorial light illuminated the large room where Mass was once heard, but there was no congregation there now, no Mass held on Sunday, and the wooden pews had long ago been removed for firewood, the iron foot pads still bolted to the floor.

People slept in sleeping bags on the floor, others on mattresses in some of the rooms. The travelers staying at the free house welcomed us, and because we were a couple, gave us a private corner of a room where there was a mattress on the floor. Someone gave us a sleeping bag to use, someone else gave Milicho a jacket. I was the only woman there that night, and next to us were two men, a British backpacker and an American traveling by motorcycle. The British man told us to hide our valuables and bury our money, and the biker stashed his helmet in our area for safekeeping. They warned us about thieves and about the Interpol, the international police funded by Nixon's drug war money, who were known to raid hippie hangouts, rape women, and steal money. In Latin America the army was the police, and the CIA ran the army. There was no police station to seek help from, no friendly cop on the beat to help if you were lost or assaulted.

I diligently buried my traveler's checks and passport under the floor before burrowing inside the sleeping bag. We slept with our clothes on and my cash in my pants, our packs as pillows. It was quiet there, with no noise from diesel trucks, no farts from old bus exhaust pipes. The church smelled like candle wax, unwashed skin and dirty socks. The hair on my arms prickled from the damp cold seeping through my down bag. I could feel Milicho shivering next to me, his smooth hairless skin suffering from the chill.

When loud shouting woke us up in the pitch-black night, I scrambled to pull on my poncho while Milicho grabbed his jacket. A group of policemen with M16 rifles and faces filled with stupidity and greed crashed into the room and ordered us to get out of bed. These were Mestizo men from the Sierra who worked for Interpol and reveled in the power that gave them. They ordered us up against the wall, grabbed the backpacks from the Europeans, and took their money and cameras. They found the helmet, my bag, and the small amount of cash I had left in it as a decoy. It was all very dark and chaotic and fast. One officer grabbed Milicho, threw him down to the ground, yanked his wrists behind his back and slapped handcuffs on him.

"*¿Qué hace él aquí? ¿Estás con él?* What is he doing here? Are you with him?" one of them barked.

"*Si, Señor*, I am," I said, barely polite.

"Well, he is under arrest. *¡Está bajo arresto!*" The officer started dragging Milicho out of the room.

"*¿Por qué?*" I demanded.

"*¡Cállate!*" the officer shouted at me, and I shut up. The other policemen yelled at Milicho as they pushed him down the hall.

"*¿Por qué estás aquí? ¿Por qué estás con la gringa? ¡No puedes estar aquí!* Why are you here? Why are you with the gringa? You can't be here!" They spoke gruffly in the guttural accent of the highlands, so violent and different from the soft language of the coast.

"Leave him alone!" I yelled. "*¡Por favor, déjalo!*"

But they ignored me and Milicho disappeared out of the room with two soldiers. An older policeman who was the officer in charge grabbed my arm, pulled me out of the room and pushed me quickly down a dark corridor, where no sound could travel. He did not ask for my money or search for drugs, as he backed me up against the cold plaster wall. He knew I knew what he wanted.

He asked me in a low growl, "Why are you with that *mono negrito*? You know what you can do. *Hagalo, y tu mono es libre.* Do it and your black monkey boyfriend goes free," he said as he pushed me harder against the wall. He was short, overweight, and stunk of decaying teeth.

Oh, no, I thought. *No way. This is not going to happen.*

Was this room, this dark hallway, this brute breathing in my face, was this what it had all come to? Was this the end of my adventure, the punishment for my bad decisions? They could shoot Milicho with impunity. They could rape me and laugh about it later. I was losing control of my post-college jaunt down the Gringo Trail. Had I been playacting as Catalina La Gringita, so in love and living in paradise? If so, the play was ending and shit suddenly got very, very real.

This was not the first time I had heard those words — *You know what you can do* — spoken as a taunt. I was nineteen years old, flying back to Oakland at the end of Thanksgiving break. I was in a taxi in the middle of the night without cash, planning to get money to pay when I got home. The cab driver turned around and said with a low sneer, "I know how you can pay your fare." I tried to act the little girl, appealing to his sense of decency, hoping that he didn't want to rape a young virgin. It didn't work. He was suddenly so overtaken by this opportunity, this porno fantasy, that he forced himself on me in the back seat.

He finished quickly, then lay on top of me and started to cry and apologize. I remember thinking about that: what life he had, family, work, driving a taxi for the rent, and then in an instant losing himself and doing damage. I felt sorrier for the cabdriver than for myself. I never reported it, feeling ashamed and thinking it was my fault for stupidly traveling without cash and putting myself in that situation. I even lied to my parents when I had to get an abortion because of it, telling them it was a guy I met at a party, not a rape.

Now here I was again, pinned down by the power of a powerless man. The Interpol officer who dragged me down the hall into this room, what life did he have outside of his uniform? Was he married, a father, a son? His job was probably the only thing bringing him up from the dirt in one of the poorest countries on the planet. He was face to face with an American girl with lots of cash, an air of entitlement, and the audacity to fuck a negrito monkey.

I stiffened and calmed my breathing, with a tone of disdain concealing my fear. I made no attempt to negotiate, play on his sympathies, ask how he would feel if it was his daughter. Not this time. This time I found my voice, and my anger. My Spanish accent was pure Ecuadorian and what emerged out of my mouth, a gringa hippie, confused him. I kicked into overdrive, feeling my way around him, using my smarts and his stupidity to my advantage.

"You are making a big mistake," I said as he pushed me against the cold wall. "*Cuidado,* watch out. You have no idea who you are dealing with, no idea!" I raised my voice. "*¡Mi padre trabaja en la embajada de Los Estados!* My father works for the embassy. This will be a *huge* mistake for you."

Once again, I yelled out names of embassy officials, politicians and prominent bankers I remembered from Philip Agee's book about the CIA. These were names I knew he knew and who, I was asserting, would find out what he was about to do. It was working, like it worked those months back with the pendejo border policeman. He stepped back, and without letting go of my arm, walked me back to the room.

The other officers brought Milicho into the room, still handcuffed, his body shivering with cold. He said nothing and did not look me in the eyes. The officer in charge ordered the men to let Milicho go. They removed the handcuffs, gathered up the cash and property they stole from us, and left.

I sat down on the mattress and cried. "Milicho! We are safe! The soldiers left. *¿Estás ok?*"

But we were never going to be okay again. The humiliation that Milicho felt was not just from being cuffed, dragged off or arrested, but from being saved by me. That was the moment our love affair began to crumble.

Milicho did not say a word or even look at me. I reached toward him to give him a hug and he moved away. We packed what little we had left, dug up the passport and money, and left Guapulo for Quito.

Milicho got on the bus down to the coast and back to Atacames while I went to the embassy to get my visa. I needed to stay in Quito a few days more, in a cheap pensión near the center, vowing never to go back to the Hotel Gran Casino.

When I got back to Atacames, Milicho was there in the casita, but our life together would never be the same. He spent more and more time away from me, away from the casita, and my loneliness grew.

CHAPTER 35:

AGUARDIENTE

Late afternoon in Atacames was not my favorite time of day. I liked the mornings, early dawn, when the air was fresh and somewhat cool after the night rain, but evenings were damp and dark, with no electricity in town and only lanterns for light, and afternoons were just muggy, heavy with mosquitoes and fatigue. No one was busy in the afternoon; the fishing canoes were docked, the comedors finished with meals, and doors closed for siesta. It was just too fucking hot to do anything but go inside where it was cooler and drink or sleep.

One of those sluggish afternoons, I sat on the floor of the casita, lit a citronella candle and a joint to keep the mosquitoes away, and waited for Milicho.

Maybe he's at the beach at Señora Inez's, I thought. *Maybe I should go there and find him.* He'd said he would come home after fishing, but that was hours ago.

It was starting to rain, hard, an *aguacera,* a sudden downpour. I did not want to stay there alone getting eaten alive by mosquitoes and debated going over to Chino's sister Columbia's house to hang out while she fed her kids, or across the bridge to the beach to hang out with the gringos.

It had been a few months since we got back from Quito, and our life had changed. Last time there was an aguacera in the afternoon, it was so sweet. Milicho and I stayed inside for hours making puka shell necklaces and rolling joints, making love on the mats. Now I was alone, and he did not come back to be with me.

That's it. I'm going to the salon. He's probably there with the muchachos.

I grabbed a long-sleeved shirt to hold over my head and jumped down off the porch onto the muddy sand outside, a flashlight in my pocket for the dark walk back. As I turned the corner onto the plaza, I heard the scratchy tape recording of cumbia played at high volume on those bad speakers. No one was dancing; it was too hot. I remembered the first time Milicho brought me there on that Saturday evening of our first date. At first it was fun and new, my life as a local, Milicho's *novia*, his gringa Catalina. I went everywhere I could with him, to *futbol* games in neighboring villages, canoe trips to the shrimp boats, and to the salon, where I learned to dance salsa and cumbia on Saturday nights.

Now Milicho spent more time with los muchachos: Chino, Clodo and the other young men I knew in Atacames. They sat at wooden tables on hard benches in the salon for hours into the evening, drinking *trago*, their drink of aguardiente with warm beer chasers or Coke, until they became completely falling-down drunk. Aguardiente is a form of cane alcohol, clear, strong, nasty and cheap. It is fire down the throat and warm coals in the stomach; it smells like paint remover and tastes like hot gasoline. This trago is rough and sad. It's the drink of the poor and hopeless. It's the drink of the men in the Andes who sing laments in tearful loud voices as they stagger up the mountain paths, fall asleep on the side of the road, and freeze to death overnight.

Some men, like Chino's father, never lost the redness in their eyes from years of drinking this rotgut stuff. Men drank and got violent. They argued loudly about stupid things; they hit their women and got into fistfights. One man burned all his wife's clothing in a drunken jealous rage. This kind of drunkenness is angry, sullen, and dark, not fun and bubbly. It is not too much red wine over a great dinner, mimosas with champagne at brunch, or Absolut on the rocks at happy hour.

There were rarely any women drinking at the tables with the men. It was a separate thing, this ritual of inebriation. The women had a trago now and then, especially at the Saturday night dances, but they had other things to do, like take care of everything in the village: the children, meals and houses. They did not have time to drink themselves into a stupor on a muggy afternoon in the salon.

Many late afternoons I sat with the muchachos into the muggy evenings and watched them drink until they put their heads down on the table and passed out. I learned to drink it a bit myself, but I could never get past the first few disgusting sips and never got to the point of drunkenness.

When I got to the salon that afternoon, I stepped into the darkened room and squinted to make out the faces of the men at the tables.

"Milicho, I thought you were coming home? *¿Por qué no vayas conmigo?*"

Milicho looked up at me then continued drumming his hands on the table, singing, "*Yo no soy marinero, soy capitán, soy capitán.*"

Chino sat across from him, his red eyes half closed, a smirk on his face. He looked like his father Don Rogelio, thin, taller than most, eyes permanently red from drinking.

"*Catalina La O!*" Clodoveo sang out a popular cumbia. He jumped around with the energy of a futbol player. The other muchacho at the table, Cabeza Loco, looked up at me briefly.

"*¿Quieres un trago?*" he slurred and handed me a glass of aguardiente. Cabeza Loco was the biggest pothead in Atacames and the biggest dealer.

I was still standing. There were no other women in the salon, except for Begner, who owned the bar and stood behind the counter pouring aguardiente from tall glass bottles with no labels. Milicho did not say a word. He took another sip from the warm Coke in his hand, chasing down the trago, and drummed on the table.

"*Ay, Catalina.*" Chino's low raspy voice beckoned me to sit down.

"*Milicho, ¿por qué no vengas conmigo a la casa?*" I asked again.

The finger drumming continued. I sat down while Chino poured me a shot.

"God, that's horrible!" I said in English, my lip curled against the awful alcohol. "How can you drink this shit?" No need to translate, my face said it all.

The muchachos laughed and passed me a bottle of warm Coke. Here I was again, another afternoon into the evening, waiting for Milicho to get up and go home. I looked around the salon at the men passed out, their heads on the tables, or having some kind of argument about stupid things. The muchachos were not married yet, and had no children, but they followed their fathers' footsteps into the salon every afternoon.

The truth was, Milicho preferred to drink with his *compañeros* than be home with me. I was supposed to be with the other women, busy with children and cooking and cleaning.

What am I doing here? I thought. *This is ridiculous. Maybe I should just leave and go home.*

I wished I could get drunk so I could find out what was so fun about drinking and sitting for hours. My ass was already sore from sitting on the wooden bench and I was bored to death and lonely as hell. I sat across the table from Milicho, waiting, my untouched glass in front of me, glancing up now and then to catch his eye and get the signal to leave. I started fidgeting, holding the bottle of Coke with both hands. Chino said something that got everyone laughing and I laughed along at whatever the joke was, a joke I did not understand in a place where I had no place.

The women had wised up long ago and stopped waiting for their men to drink up and go home. They stopped waiting for them altogether. I, on the other hand, kept thinking Milicho would rather be with me and make love to me, the way he used to, not sit around in dark, dank bar, listening to scratchy cumbia on the tape recorder and singing along to boleros filled with lyrics of loss and sorrow.

The rain was slowing now but the humidity still sat on the air like a wet sponge.

"*Ya me voy,*" I said out loud, hopelessly, too sad to be angry, and walked out of the salon into the darkness, the voice of Judy Collins singing the same phrase over and over in my head: *Wasn't it a long way down? Isn't it a long way down?*

At the casita, I smoked the rest of a joint and listened to the tape of Linda Ronstadt that I brought with me from home, playing "Heart Like a Wheel," a song filled with lyrics of loss and sorrow, on the small cassette player Milicho found for me while I waited for his body to crash through the door and pass out on the floor, stinking drunk.

"Some say the heart is just like a wheel.
When you bend it, you can't mend it.
But my love for you is like a sinking ship
and my heart is on that ship out on the ocean.
And it's only love, and it's only love
That can take a human being and turn him inside out."

CHAPTER 36:

MAL OJO

For the next few weeks, I stayed on the beach with Señora Inez most of the day. Milicho was not around that much during the days, and he often came back very late at night. We had not made love in weeks. I was getting worse, more frail, from the dysentery that had plagued me for months. Señora Inez said I had *mal ojo*, evil eye, and that it was mal ojo that was making me sick.

"Be serious," I snorted. "I'm sick because of dysentery, not evil eye."

"*Mal Ojo*," she said. "You need to be cured."

What I need are the right drugs and a good, clean hospital, I thought.

Señora Inez clicked her tongue against her toothless upper gums and turned back to the pot of rice cooking on the coals. She continued mumbling to herself as I lay down on the hammock strung between two coconut palms outside her casita. The breeze off the ocean kept the mosquitoes away and the palm fronds clattered against each other far above.

I had become sicker over the last few months, dropping weight too fast. I could not eat anything without getting the shits. Even a diet of rice and bananas went right through me. I knew it was getting serious. I had little strength, my skin was sallow, my stools hot liquid and yellow. I had to do something before I wasted away completely, but it was hard to think of leaving paradise. The mere thought of taking the trip exhausted me. It would be an hour to get to Esmeraldas, then an eight-hour bus ride up to Quito, then a ten-hour flight through Mexico to LA. It seemed impossible. I was too sick.

I dismissed the idea of a hospital in Quito, having heard too many horror stories of botched surgeries and dirty needles. Perhaps Señora

Inez could help. She was a *curandera*, a medicine woman, and people trusted the curanderas more than the medical doctors. I heard stories of sick children taken out of the hospital and brought to curanderos where they were treated with herbs and potions and got better. If local people brought their children to her for herbs and cures, why shouldn't I?

I'm being ridiculous, I thought. *What I have is amoebic dysentery and I need drugs.*

"*Ojo*," she said again as she passed by the hammock to fill the bucket at the well, shaking her head. She had been saying this for weeks.

"*Hable en serio.* Be serious," I said. "I'm sick, not cursed!"

I never questioned what Señora Inez meant by "having ojo." I thought it was just the superstition of the local people, descendants of Africans and Indians. I not only rejected it as silly and superstitious but discounted the depth and seriousness of her charges. I never questioned why I got sick because my modern mind thought it already knew. It was the germs, dirty water, worms, and bacteria in the milk and cheese. My immune system was worn out by pabulum, antibiotics, pasteurized milk, and frozen vegetables.

Some people thought I gave mal ojo to others. They said it when the litter of puppies on a nearby farm suddenly died a few days after I played with them. La gringita gave them mal ojo, they said. She looked at them too intently, they said. A few months earlier, Señora Elena's two young sons were taken for a joyride in a car on the beach and died when the car flipped over in the soft sand. I didn't see that these events could have any connection to me; they were the consequence of tropical bacteria and bad luck, but maybe ojo energy was all around me and that's why I was getting infections. Illness continually invaded my body: a staph infection, lice, and the dysentery that had taken a turn for the worse. I lay in the hammock, so exhausted I was a bit delirious.

Maybe Señora Inez is telling me I need to be cured of mal ojo not only to save my life, but to correct the life of the village as well.

I was having crazy visions of a village out of balance, with a weakened immune system, vulnerable to bad energy caused by me. Maybe I was causing these tragedies just by being there. I was white, rich, unmarried, and childless. They probably wondered what I was doing there, why I was choosing to live in a bamboo hut with no water, electricity or toilet.

No wonder they are suspicious. Maybe I do ask too many questions. Perhaps this is what they mean by mal ojo.

Soon I became too incapacitated to get out of the hammock. I had nothing to lose. I could not make the journey out of Atacames, so I surrendered to the curandera.

"*Ok Señora, dime qué hacer y lo hare.* Tell me what to do and I'll do it."

"*Bueno.*" She told me that every morning for the next three days I had to go to Señora Marguerita's farm and bring back a newly laid egg from her chickens.

"*¿Qué?* You must be kidding!" I said. The farm was at least three miles inland. "I can't walk that far! I can barely make it here from my house across the footbridge!"

"*Hagalo,* do it," she said. "*Sola.* You must do it by yourself."

That first morning, I walked slowly down the beach and then into the campo, squatting along the way when the runs hit me, kicking sand over the hot yellow puddles. It took me hours, having to rest several times along the way. I trudged back with the egg slowly, the late morning sun already making the sand dangerously hot.

Señora Inez had me take off my clothes and stand in the middle of the palapa. I was too exhausted to worry about anyone seeing me naked. She wrapped an old, frayed cloth tape-measure ribbon around my bust as if measuring for a bra, marked where it closed, then folded it up and put it on top of my head in one direction then the other like a cross. She touched it in cross directions on my forehead and shoulders, my wrist, forearms and back, and last on my heart. Then she unfolded the ribbon and marked with a pen the place on the tape where the ends met. She rolled up the tape like a snake and set it aside.

Next, she took the egg and rubbed it slowly and methodically all over my naked body, chanting low to herself in a language that was not Spanish. I stood a bit unsteadily, grateful for the breeze coming through the palms. The egg was cool and soothing on my hot skin. She started on top of my head, wiping my eyes, chest, arms from shoulder to hands, stomach, belly button, legs. When she finished, she broke the egg into a half glass of water, swirled it around a bit, and peered at the yolk. The white of the egg rose to the top like it was cooked. She set the glass aside, then repeated the measurement around my breasts, only this time the tape did not close. There was a gap between the end of the tape and the marked spot where it had closed before. I saw it with my own eyes; there was no reason the tape measurement would be different, but it was. Señora Inez measured the width of the gap with her fingers. It was as wide as her two fingers held together.

"*Dos dedos.* You are two-fingered *ojeada,*" she said, clicking her tongue again and shaking her head.

"Is that bad?"

"That is a lot, *mucho ojo.*" She told me to rest and come back in the morning with another egg. I rested in the hammock until the day cooled a bit, then made my way slowly down the beach and across the bridge to my casita, exhausted.

The next morning, I went to get the second egg. Again, it took me hours to walk down the beach and to Marguerite's farm, stopping often to rest. I was a little delirious from the walk back from the farm as I stood naked in the middle of the palapa, wobbling back and forth. Señora Inez again measured me with the ribbon but did not look at it. She rubbed the egg over my skin again and broke the egg in another glass, studied it, and sent me off to rest in the hammock.

The third day I made the same journey, and she did the same ritual. I thought how far I had come from who I was and what I had known, standing naked in a palapa on a beach at the center of the globe while an old toothless woman in a housedress and sandals performed ancient African rituals to rid my body of evil eye. When Señora Inez measured me again, at the end of the third egg ritual, the tape ends overlapped more than an inch over the marked spot.

"*Bueno, pues.* That should hold you for a while," she said as she put the tape away and started brewing some coffee. She sent me to rest in the hammock and somehow, I made it back across the bridge that afternoon.

The next morning, I woke up strangely energetic. My stools were hard and brown, my eyes clear, my skin pink.

I can't believe this. How is this happening? I feel completely well!

I tried to think of the reasons for my apparent recovery. Was the dysentery just subsiding for a while, like it sometimes did? But the diarrhea had never gone away before so completely and I hadn't had this amount of energy for months. I could not explain it away. The curandera healed me; I believed it to be true, and I was grateful for it.

Milicho came in from his morning fishing and was startled to see me so alert. I told him what had been going on, but he was not surprised. I guess he had seen this before; he knew the power of his mother's healing. I was able to walk at a normal pace all the way to Señora Inez's casita. My tongue tasted fresh, and I ate a meal of baked plátano and eggs, the first real food I had been able to eat in a while. I even went for a swim. That night I went to the bar and danced cumbia with Don Enrique.

For the first time in months, I was not afraid. I was utterly and completely well, for about three days. Then I relapsed sicker than before. My fear returned with my illness and this time I knew I had to get out of there or I was going to die for sure.

That is the trouble with mal ojo. It is a fierce energy in constant combat with the energy of healing. Ojo is tricky; it fools people and then it wins. Children who were taken out of hospitals and brought to curanderas were made miraculously well, but the cure did not last. The energy of the curandera's healing lasted sometimes only for a few days, and then, deep in the jungle, far from the hospital, the children died. Señora Inez rid my body of mal ojo for three short days, but she could not cure me completely.

I told Milicho and Señora Inez I had to go home, that I needed to get treatment, and that I would be back as soon as I could. I was preparing to leave Atacames, to go to Quito to wait for money to be wired for a plane ticket, then back to California.

"*¡Ay, Catalina! No te vayas,*" Señora Inez said this as a sigh as she prepared her breakfast at the sand table, rolling the charred plátanos into the coals and boiling water for coffee. "*No te vayas,*" she said. "Don't go.

You won't be healed. They don't know how to heal you. *Los gringos no saben nada. Nada de ojo.*" She said they will give me drugs that will kill my insides and do nothing to get rid of the mal ojo. She told me she could heal me for good if I was open to it. But I was not; I was resistant.

"I have to go," I said. "I'm afraid I am going to die if I stay."

"*Puedes morir si te vas.* You may die if you leave," she replied in a low voice.

Señora Inez turned her back on me, shaking her head and mumbling to herself. I watched as she walked out of the casita towards the well to get water for the rice. When she came back, she walked past me without seeing me, as if I was already gone. Señora Inez did not believe I would leave and come back. Where I came from was unimaginably distant to Señora Inez, and to Milicho, for that matter. When I told him I was going back to California, I might as well have told him I was going to Mars, the cost of the ticket more than people there made in a lifetime.

"*No te preocupes. Vuelvo en tres meses,*" I said quite nonchalantly. "Don't worry, I'll be back in three months." He must have thought I was crazy or worse, lying.

"*Los gringos no vuelven.* Gringos don't come back," he said.

That last day before I left, we swam out past the breakers into the calm water. The water was so clear and blue and Milicho was exquisitely beautiful, the sunlight sparkling on his black hair, his dark skin glistening. I wanted to capture that moment forever, and even though I planned to come back, I had a sense of foreboding, a feeling that somehow, I was letting it go. We had stopped making love when I got so sick, but that last night we lay in each other's arms like before.

We had fallen in love in the casita. We talked of our lives and learned to be naked in front of each other, no closet or bathroom there to give us privacy. We fought in the casita and cried on the mats, stomped out the doorway, yelled angrily through the open glassless windows. The mat on the floor hurt our bodies when the loving was not gentle. When it rained a hard aguacera, the noise on the tin roof was at times astounding and fun, at other times relentless, disturbing our sleep and making the roaches scurry around fretfully from the pounding noise.

Sometimes the casita filled up with the aroma of the tropical flowers in the garden, sometimes with the stench of too much aguardiente and pot, or of too much anger and hurt, too much sweat and longing.

And then we left the casita and left each other.

I thought that life would always be there, that I would come back to the casita and to Milicho, that it would not disappear into a dream.

CHAPTER 37:

LOS ANGELES

I sat at the kitchen table at my parents' new house in Los Angeles, the one they moved into after I left. It was a beautiful English Tudor on the edge of Hancock Park in midtown Los Angeles. To me it was a palace, its walls, floors and ceilings so substantial, thick, and solid. I felt the strange comfort of carpet on my bare feet and the support of a good mattress under my hip bones. I touched the glass in the windows, the tile in the bathroom, attempting to ground myself. The bathroom was the biggest shock: it was inside the house, enclosed and clean, with mauve pile carpet and a toilet with a seat, soft two-ply paper in the holder. This was really all I needed to live: the cleanliness, closeness and privacy of a toilet.

When my father picked me up at the airport he walked right by me, not recognizing me, now thirty pounds thinner, sallow, and dressed like a bedraggled street hippie. For once in my life, he told me I was too thin. I laughed at the irony of that.

When my doctor called me with my stool test results, he yelled into the phone, "Where the hell have you been?"

I stayed in their house for three months, taking Flagyl, a strong drug to cure the amoebic dysentery that was killing my insides. By March, I was finally able to eat normally and had enough energy to swim in the pool. I knew things were back to normal when I sat down for breakfast at the kitchen table while my mother fixed me a bagel and coffee.

"Eating bagels now, are we? You better watch it." My father was still commenting on my eating, even after I had almost died.

I didn't care; I was healthy enough to eat real food, which meant I was healthy enough to return to Ecuador. My parents didn't even try to dissuade me from going back, much to my relief. I wrote to Milicho almost daily, getting only one short letter in return. I chalked up his lack of communication to the slow, unreliable mail system in Ecuador, ignoring any other reason he did not write me back.

I was so wrapped up in my relationship and my life in Atacames that I failed to see what was happening with my parents. One week before my departure, it was my mother's birthday, and we were all going to a restaurant for dinner that evening. In the afternoon, my mother came home, walked into her bedroom and braced her arms against the mirrored maple dresser, the one they had owned since their wedding. Her face was like nothing I had ever seen before: not pain, not disdain, not even fear or exhaustion. This was different; this was stone, ashen, steel, dead anger. I could not ignore it; it was too big. I started to walk toward her. She did not look up. She stood, bent over, holding herself up against the dresser, as if she had lost her breath.

"Not now!" she said fiercely, and I backed up and closed the bedroom door.

Later my mother came into my room, still unable to speak. She had not spoken up during her marriage. She did not speak of the detaching of her husband from her, of his absences, his love affair with another, his humiliation of her. She did not speak of this even to her sister, her closest friend in life, the sister who had married her husband's brother. And now in their thirty-sixth year of marriage, her husband could not speak either and handed her a letter instead. The letter was handwritten, in that particular script everyone in the family had come to recognize with trepidation or excitement, holding words he could not speak directly, words of love, of advice, of pride or criticism. I knew these letters well, and my stomach gripped when my mother handed the familiar envelope to me.

"Here, read it," she said, not looking up.

Dear Gerry... it began, and it told of his decision to leave her for his thirty-year-old receptionist. He handed her a letter to that effect a few days before her fifty-fifth birthday and shortly before my takeoff.

I tried to talk to my mother about what had happened.

"I don't want to talk about it," my mother said in her metallic raspy voice. Cancer had ripped out her pharynx, destroyed her voice, the voice that could sell anything, that hawked her wares in department stores, spoke in lilting French, gave political speeches, that could do anything except sing. I am convinced her voice was destroyed by not speaking her rage. She swallowed her anger, ate her humiliation, shut herself behind stone. She bottled it in, and it attacked her thyroid, her lymph glands and her throat. After the cancer surgery, she spoke with metallic sounds, devoid of human tenor, frightening her baby granddaughter who screamed and squirmed out of her arms.

I wanted only to return to Ecuador. I was hopeful, in love, and wanted to run out of the house before it collapsed around me, crushing me with the weight of silence, loneliness, disappointment and pain. My mother's anger was so deep she had swallowed it whole; she could not move, and she could not be reached.

I moved about the house with thoughts in Spanish, humming Milicho's song, the one he sang when he played drums on his thigh. "*Yo no soy marinero, soy capitán, soy capitán.*" I gathered my things together — fresh clothes, books, a cassette player, my guitar, clothes for Señora Inez and the girls, colorful skirts, sandals, walking shoes. I was not bringing a backpack this time, only a suitcase. This time, I was not going as a tourist, I was going there to live.

I could not speak to my father that evening in the restaurant. I hated him in that moment, not for deciding to leave, but for being too cowardly to have spoken the truth to her directly, for merely handing her a letter. For being too cowardly not to have left sooner, before the cancer, before my mother was too sick to begin a new life. I also hated him in that moment for ruining my own illusion of love. I had not wanted to see or hear the truth, and no one tried to tell me, so I paid no attention. Now I was learning the truth in familiar handwriting, and I wanted to pretend I no longer understood English.

I called Eduardo, my Ecuadorian American friend in Esmeraldas, to ask about the muchachos and tell him I was coming in a few days. He was hesitant, sounding strange on the phone.

"Are you sure you want to come back?" he said.

"What do you mean? Of course I'm coming. Why? What's going on?"

"The muchachos have all gone to Quito. They have been there for a few months. Milicho isn't in Atacames."

"But he's coming back, isn't he?" I asked.

"I don't know... And I'm not sure what to say, but I think he is with another girl."

"That's crazy. I've only been gone a few months! It can't be true. Milicho wouldn't leave me!"

I put down the receiver. I was leaving the next day to go back to Atacames forever. *Eduardo must be wrong about this*, I thought. *How could everything change like that?* I told Milicho I was coming back in March, and I wrote letters every week. I couldn't *not* go. I already had a ticket to return to Ecuador, to Atacames, to Milicho. My father even gave me the money for the ticket.

In that moment, when the possibility of losing Milicho appeared, I knew I still had to go back. I loved the village and the life there as much as I loved Milicho. He would come back to me when I arrived, I had no doubt. I had to go back, had to get out of this house, away from this coldness and devastation.

I did not speak of any of this to my mother, not wanting to give her any more reason to ask me to stay. She was in bad shape. I half-heartedly made an offer to be with her.

"Do you want me to stay?" I asked.

"No," she said. "Go back and finish your movie."

I loved her for that. She was not talking about a real movie. She knew my life in Ecuador was something I needed to play out, and when it was finished, I would come back to my real life. I knew deep inside that she was right, but I could not admit to it. I was too involved with the drama of that moment in time.

At the airport, my mother and I did not say too much. My friend Daria was holding my mother's hand while I loaded my bags on the belt. We had an unspoken, wordless conversation through our eyes.

Don't ask me to stay.

Don't ask me if I want you to stay. And don't stay because of me, she wordlessly replied.

Don't let me go if you really need me. But what I really meant was, *Don't need me, so I can be ok about leaving.*

My mother never once revealed any desire to stop me from leaving, even though her life had been inalterably broken apart. We hid ourselves under hugs and kisses on the lips and a few distracted words of love and goodbye and write-as-soon-as-you-can as she waved me onto the plane.

As I sat down, I saw through the window where my mother and Daria stood, still holding hands, and finally I wept. She was crying, and so was I, but we could not cry in front of each other.

Was I selfish? Would I have stayed home if she had asked me to?

I had promised Milicho I would come back in three months. "Wait for me," I said, "I will be back." I knew I had to come back to him.

The lump of tears rose on departure and again on landing, but I held myself together for the flight. The last image of my mother's face filled with pain, which I saw through the airplane window, was still in my mind. I knew I should be closer; I knew I was needed.

But it was bad timing, and I needed to leave.

CHAPTER 38:

QUITO

I arrived in Quito with a screaming headache from landing at 9,500 feet, and a feeling of unease.

I rested in the apartment of a family friend who welcomed me when I arrived. I could not understand why Milicho had come there. He hated Quito and had nothing but bad luck there. It did not make sense. The muchachos would never leave *paraiso* in the winter for no reason.

Winter on the coast was the rainy season, the cold season, the season of malaria and tetanus. The water made everything grow uncontrolled: vines, trees, bananas, mangos, bacteria, mosquitoes, cockroaches. Everything thrived on the moisture but was threatened at the same time, and death and illness came more easily in the winter, in the rain.

But winter in the Sierra was even more dangerous. The cold mixed with damp, thin air, leaving one gasping for breath. Mountain roads washed out and were often blocked by slides. Bus drivers had to back down narrow mountain passes, unable to turn the bus around.

The year before, Ellen and I were on a bus that had to back down a pass high in the Andes. The passengers gripped their seats and fumbled with their rosaries. I stared out the window at the small crosses on the side of the road marking earlier deaths from buses falling off the cliffs. No one breathed while the bus slowly inched backwards to the left and to the right. The only sounds were the creaking brakes, the shouts of "*¡Dale! ¡Dale!*" from the young boys running alongside the bus, urging the driver to keep going, and the low murmur of the collective desperate prayer.

There was little shelter in Quito, a city inhospitable to Black boys from the coast, a city filled with Indians in rough wool ruanas, bowler hats and bare feet, walking up the steep sidewalks away from the rich commercial flatlands toward the hilltop slums. Buses passed by, lumbering slowly in first gear up the steep, narrow, cobblestone streets, buses filled beyond capacity, boys hanging onto the door railings, leathered faces crammed up against the metal-framed windows. This was not a friendly place, especially in the winter, when a night spent in the streets without shelter could kill.

As soon as my headache subsided, I went out looking for Milicho. He was somewhere in this city, and I stared out the taxi window looking for him.

The muchachos should not be that hard to find, I thought. I was nervous, uneasy, but also excited to see him. *It will all work out*, I silently prayed.

This was a sudden jump from LA, yet Quito did not seem strange. Maybe I really was coming to another home. But it felt desolate without the connection with Milicho and the thought of our not being together made me very, very sad.

I walked to the Avenida Amazonas where tourists and wealthy people sat at outdoor cafés. I had a hunch the boys were here to score and sell, make some *plata*, some cash, to live on for a while.

I walked up and down Amazonas for a day or so until I ran into a guy who had been in Atacames and knew the muchachos.

"All the boys are in Quito," he said. "Chino, Clodoveo, some other cousins."

"Why? What are they doing here?"

"*Negocio.*" By business, he meant weed.

He led me to an apartment in Quito where they were staying. I wondered why, if they came here to buy weed, they didn't go to Colombia instead? And why sell it in Quito and not in Atacames? Something was weird, out of place.

When I walked into the apartment, Milicho was sitting in one of the back rooms and he suddenly jumped up and told me to leave.

"*¡Quitate, Cata*, get out!" No warm embraces here, no glad surprised smiles, only harsh fear in his voice. "*Mal momento.* This is not a good time," he said breathlessly, avoiding my eyes.

He continued talking rapidly and I could not process what he was saying or the look in his eyes, and then suddenly I understood. The other muchachos who were in the apartment, Tarzan and Cabeza Loca, were moving frantically around in the other room when suddenly the police came in. I stood in the hallway, my head bursting with jet lag, altitude sickness, disbelief and confusion. Before I realized what was going on, the three were arrested. What started out as a bad feeling, a weird hunch that something was wrong, turned out to be true.

The police ignored me as they dragged the boys out of the apartment. They were taken to a decrepit, filthy jail in Ambato, a town north of Quito, and charged with car theft. They had been in the middle of a dope deal, and the deal fell through. The buyer would not pay and ran off, leaving them in his car, which turned out to be stolen. They could not tell the police why they were in the car, so they took the rap for car theft, which was a whole lot better than drug dealing.

How did I come to learn all this? From Maria, Milicho's new girlfriend. She was not in the apartment when the police came but arrived later with Chino and Clodoveo. Maria was about my age, with a pretty face, heavy boned and slightly overweight. She was from Colombia and spoke very good English. She had been an exchange student somewhere in the States and had a five-year-old daughter from a previous relationship. Now she and I were thrown together, trying to get the boy we both loved out of jail.

From the moment I stood in the middle of that dark apartment while the *federales* with guns drawn cuffed and hauled away the love of my life, I was cuffed by my own bad judgment. I should have just turned on my heels and gone back to LA. Instead, I could not accept this new reality. I moved into "Miss Fix-It" mode and spent the next five days and a couple of thousand dollars paying off every level of cop, prosecutor, jailer, and official needed to get the boys out of jail. The days were exercises in frustration. Lawyers, *policía, secretarias*, local officials: they all looked like used car salesmen or bozos, with overly formal language and slimy demeanors. The whole Atacames family was involved: Tarzan's sisters, Milicho's sister, and Loco's mother all came to help.

There we were, a bunch of friends and relations, getting drunk to keep from crying in the *parque* of Ambato. We were stuck dealing with a legal system short on the rights of the individual. In the States, if someone is not charged with a crime after four days, they would be released. In Ecuador, no such due process existed. The muchachos would not get out until they found Jimmie, the guy who originally stole the car, whoever the hell he was.

The muchachos were in for four days and nights, without counsel, communication, or food. In Ecuadorian jails, they did not feed the prisoners, so the families had to drop off food for their loved ones. I, La Gringita, flush with cash, installed Clodoveo in a hotel room near the jail so he could bring the boys food every day. I did everything I could to get the muchachos released, accompanied by Maria, the bilingual bitch from Colombia who stole Milicho from me while I was shitting all of Ecuador out of my ass in LA.

I was like a machine on autopilot, traveling by bus with Maria, talking about Milicho, assessing the situation, planning strategy. I put one foot in front of the other to the police station, the court, the judge, the jail, and the bank. I could not feel anything. I did not feel powerful or capable and I certainly did not feel appreciated. It was as if everyone assumed I would pay their way out. I changed so many traveler's checks into sucres to bribe the long line of officials that the Interpol became suspicious and put a tail on me. They thought I was dealing drugs, not paying off slimy men behind crappy wooden desks in the hope of saving my lover and my friends, all the while with the other woman by my side.

I was totally in limbo. The more I got to know Maria, the more I believed Milicho should be more in love with me than her. But inertia is a very strong force, and returning to me when he was already involved with someone else would be a much harder step. But I wanted him.

"Maybe I am heading for a fall," I said to no one in particular, "but I have to try. And now he's in jail, untouchable, and I am left to wonder and guess and try to keep the lid on."

I spent the week at the house in Ambato making meals with Clodo and playing cards with Chino, Mercedes, Elda, and Columbia. Everyone was there, and I felt really loved by them all, so much so that Maria came crying to Chino that everyone was against her being with Milicho.

"*La cosa es que Milicho* loves us both," I told him.

After almost a week of pleading, throwing gringo weight around, and paying a lot of cash, I got the muchachos released. Maria and I rushed to the jail and stood in the dirt courtyard near the entrance. When he was released, Milicho crossed the jail yard and came over to where Maria and I were standing. He went right into her arms, without a greeting or a thank you to me. In that moment, my heart cracked open.

Maybe he doesn't know I was the one who did this, who got him out? I thought to myself. M*aybe he does and it doesn't make any difference.*

I stood frozen with pain, standing in the reality that Milicho wanted Maria and not me.

After the muchachos were released and the families went back to Atacames, Milicho, Maria, Chino, Clodo and Cabeza Loca stayed in Quito in the apartment where I'd found them a few weeks before. I rented a room in a house nearby. The week I spent there could be entitled "Play It As It Lays." I went a little *loca*, not knowing what I was doing there, not knowing if I should stay or leave. I did anything I could to fill the hole of rejection. I slept with Clodo a few times, and had a night of sex with Chino, too angry and hurt to care what it meant. Then I had a quickie on the floor with Milicho one morning. We talked and kissed and cried in drunken *tristeza*, sadness. He told me he loved me, to wait until things calmed down. I felt ok, not upset, because I was certain we would end up together. He was the love of my life, and he would soon realize I was his. But he seemed stuck and not dealing so well.

"*Quiero ir a la playa*," I told Milicho. I wanted to go to the beach, but not everyone wanted to go back to Atacames. Chino wanted to split Quito, but Milicho wanted to stay, and Maria wanted to stay in Quito with her daughter. There was talk of a restaurant in Salinas, a trip to Baños, but it seemed that life in Atacames with them was out. I decided to go to Atacames by myself to get away from the mess.

I told them, "*Ustedes son mi familia.* But I can't stay here. I need to settle down."

My emotional life was spread out before them, yet they were hard to depend on. Maybe the heartache was worth it, though; at least I felt alive, and I had been in a state of numbness since returning from LA and needed to feel something, however painful. But in another striking moment of bad judgment, I went back — not to Los Angeles, but to Atacames. Even if Milicho was lost to me, I was going to make my life there anyway.

The day before I left, I walked towards Avenida Amazonas, past the fancy clothing shops and cafés and hotels. Clodo and Loco were up ahead. Turning the corner, two Otavalan men in the full dress of their tribe passed by me. They wore white cotton pants, deep blue ponchos, and bowler hats, their black hair braided long down their backs, their feet in tire-tread sandals. They walked among elegant men in suits and ties on their way to their offices, past the darker skinned woman sitting on a ratty blanket, infant under her poncho, with her hand outstretched holding a cup for change, and women in high heels, dressed to the nines, sipping espresso at the cafés that lined the Avenida.

I had to slow down a bit and see it all, the crazy, amazing scene going on around me.

CHAPTER 39

ATACAMES

Soon I was back in Atacames, having schlepped halfway across the hemi-sphere, landing in the village with a suitcase, a new tape player and new clothes, ready to live there forever with Milicho. But he dumped me for Maria and her adorable five-year-old daughter, who arrived in Milicho's life all potty-trained and verbal, like a rescue dog you adopt from the shel-ter after its chewing and carpet-peeing days are over. I hadn't come all that way with dreams of a tropical love life for nothing. I certainly did not want to turn around and go back to LA, where my parents were in the throes of separation and my now-famous movie star brother's name and face would be splattered all over and permeate every minute of my day. No thanks.

I arrived to an overwhelming memory of Atacames: the humidity, green plush growth, tropical wetness and heat, the sweaty faces and loud insects. I was overtaken with the *belleza*, the beauty, the first day walking toward the river, taking a good swim and a hit on a joint, and I almost cried with joy to be there. But it felt like a dream sensation, a déjà vu. I knew where I was, but it was different this time. Something about it had changed; it was distorted, unrecognizable. None of the muchachos were playing around, the oppressive heat made people a little heavy hearted. Even the jugos tasted terrible and empty.

"*Así es la vida en Atacames* for me now," I sighed as I sat on the beach one day. "I've got my cassette player, my music, a guitar, and sun. And why not? We will see what happens with Milicho." One thing I knew for sure, it would never be like before. That would be left as a perfect jewel to treasure.

I rented my own little house for a couple of bucks of month, bought a real mattress, and set up a decent charcoal sand table to heat water for coffee. I hung bananas from the ceiling but ate every meal at Señora Inez's comedor on the beach, my status as daughter-in-law having survived the breakup intact. In Atacames, the families greeted me warmly with hugs, all so grateful to me for what I had done for the muchachos.

"*¿Y tu esposo? ¿Cuándo viene?*" Everyone asked when Milicho was coming. He was still *mi esposo* as far as everyone was concerned. I didn't want to tell them the truth, that I didn't know when, or if, he was coming back or coming back to me. And to boot, Marcel, the sweet student from Cuenca whom I met last year in Atacames, was there with his guitar.

Soon everyone returned, including Clodo, Chino and Tarzan. Maria and Milicho came for Easter week then went back to Quito. I wanted to tell Milicho that if he went back to Quito with her it was over for us, but I was too scared to lay down an ultimatum. After all the watching and waiting and lovemaking and game playing, it all boiled down to one thing: He was with her. And despite the jealousy and double-standard bullshit and anger, despite my sex with Chino or anyone else, it came down to the fact that I still loved him. Despite his arrogance and immaturity, lovemaking with anyone else felt like just fucking. I could try to explain it away with my head, use my anger at his audacious sexism to pull me out of the depths, but it did nothing to stop the pain. Never depend on someone else for emotional support: That was the lesson I was learning. Don't lean, because the stick will eventually break.

Milicho and Maria and the little screamer did return a month later and moved into a casita next to mine, as if that was ok, as if it meant we had all moved on. But I had not, and Milicho's actions only added to my confusion. I could hear Maria call out Milicho's name when he came in through my window to have a nice breakup screw. For once I was glad there was no glass in the windows, or screens for that matter. But how often can one legitimately have breakup sex? Is it considered breakup sex when it keeps happening, or does it then get recharacterized as cheating on your current girlfriend with your ex?

"*No me escribiste.* You didn't write to me. *Creí que nunca volverías.* I thought you were never coming back." Milicho told me this one afternoon when we sat together in the salon.

"*¿Qué dice? ¡Te escribí! ¡Bastante!* What do you mean? I wrote to you every week! Of course, I was coming back. Why wouldn't I? *Y volví*, didn't I? I did come back!"

Milicho blamed me for deserting him, for going off to the States just like that.

"*¡No había letras! ¡Mentirosa!* There were no letters. You are lying!" Milicho got up and walked out of the salon.

"I was only away for three months!" I yelled after him. "*¡Tres meses!* That wasn't so long to wait, *si me amaras*, if you loved me!"

"*¡Si me amaras, me habrías escrito!* If you loved me, you would have written," he screamed back, almost at the plaza. "*Si me amaras, no te hubieras ido.* If you loved me, you would not have left in the first place!"

That was it, wasn't it? I should not have left. No matter that I was wasting away with dysentery and jaundice and staph infections. No matter that my hair was falling out from the gasoline Señora Inez put on my head to kill the lice. No matter that I had lost thirty pounds in two months and could not walk across the footbridge without collapsing. I thought I was dying. I needed to get out of there and get well, something I thought was fairly obvious.

"*Nunca dudé que volvería*, I never doubted I would come back, and I never doubted my love for you."

A few weeks later, I found out it was the pregnant woman at the post office who ruined my life and took Milicho away from me. I wrote him letters once a week for three months. I wrote in my best Spanish, professing my love and counting the days until I was on my way back to him. I got one letter from him: one paragraph in childlike print with no punctuation, and then nothing. But that was ok; I knew it was more difficult to get mail out of Ecuador than to receive it. I also knew he did not read or write that much in his life, so I was not surprised by the childlike spelling. I assumed he was getting all my letters, and I was really upset when I found out the truth.

The son of the woman who ran the post office came over one day and gave me a box filled with letters. His mother had been very pregnant when I left for California, and when she delivered her baby, she simply stopped delivering the mail. It wasn't until several months later that she had the time and strength to clean up her house and found all my letters, all addressed to Milicho, that he never got.

"*¡Mira!* I did write to you, see?" I said as I showed him the pile of mail.

But it was too late to undo the hurt and take back our words, too late to start over.

CHAPTER 40:

EARTHQUAKE

An earthquake rocked the coast one night just before dawn, the epicenter very close. I was alone in my new house and suddenly it began to shake violently. I awoke immediately, familiar with the rolling sensation of an earthquake, having spent my life in California.

This was a strong one. The tiny salamanders that lived in the slats of the bamboo started scurrying around. The house swayed like palm fronds in the wind, the stilts holding it up shifted in circles in the soft sand. I stayed on my mattress, no need to jump under tables or run under doorjambs. There was nothing that could really fall and hurt me, no concrete or bricks or wood beams or glass, only bamboo and tin roofing. There was no electricity to go out, no breakers to flip, no water pipes to burst, no gas main to turn off, no dishes to break, no TV to fall on my head. I lit a kerosene lantern and felt quite safe.

A few years earlier, I clung to my bed while it rocked during the 1971 Sylmar earthquake in LA. I shared the apartment with my cousin Nancy, and we rode our beds like bucking-bronco riders, holding on until the shaking stopped. Then we ran outside the building onto the street as fast as we could. In the predawn darkness we met our neighbors for the first time. Here in Atacames, I lived alone. There was no phone call to await or make, as Nancy and I did, betting on whose mother would call first.

In the first few moments after the quake settled, I felt strangely calm. I got up and opened the wooden windows as I heard my name called.

"*¿Catalina?¿Estás bien?*"

"*Sí,*" I answered to the small group of men walking outside. "*Toda tranquilla.*"

They had their lanterns lit and were going door to door making sure everyone was ok. They were checking up on me, knew me by name.

Don't see that happen much in LA, I thought.

As the light grew, I went outside and saw there was a huge crack in the path right outside my house. The crevasse was two feet wide and several yards long, as if the village had split along one of its seams. The epicenter was out in the ocean and there was talk of a tsunami, but none came. Had there been one, there was nothing that would have prevented the houses, the footbridge, perhaps the village itself from washing away. I wondered what would have happened if the crack had been under my house. I also wondered what it would be like if groups of neighbors walked up and down the streets of LA after an earthquake, checking up on the inhabitants of the houses, knowing them by name, calling out to see if everyone was ok.

Later that day, I sat in the hammock at Señora Inez's, the sun gorgeous and the day perfect. But Atacames, so idyllic and peaceful, seemed not as stable as it had the day before. The beach seemed to have shifted a little, and there was a sense of risk in the breeze. The only major damage was in Esmeraldas, where the concrete buildings were badly damaged. The new concrete school building fell down, but thankfully no one was hurt because it was 4:00 a.m. when the quake hit. Had it been a few hours later, an entire generation would have been wiped out. God does like to send messages, it seemed.

Impermanence was a fact of life in the tropics, and the buildings that tried to be permanent, those of concrete and brick, tumbled to the ground or washed out to sea. Ecuador was a poor country, and the infrastructure was as flimsy as the roots of tropical trees. It was important not to have too many things there. Keep it simple, because what you have may be gone in an instant, by earthquake or tsunami or hurricane. If the inhabitants dared to live too close to the ocean, someday someone would matter of factly tell a visitor that there once was a village there, but the waves took it.

**

So began my life in Atacames alone, the only gringa in residence. I spent a lot of time by myself, writing in my journals, playing Joni Mitchell and Linda Ronstadt tapes over and over, especially Joni's song of yearning for California. I learned some boleros on my guitar and latched on to any gringo tourists that passed through. Milicho continued to give me hope that we would be together again.

"Wait for me just a little while longer. *Tenga paciencia.* I'm going to leave Maria, but I just can't do it yet."

Milicho said this and I believed him for a long time. In fact, I believed that he loved me, and all that other stuff was merely a distraction, an unfortunate necessity. Maria was something he had to do because he'd gotten himself so entangled he could not quite get it back the way it was. I suspected some kind of insidious business they may have been in together, drug dealing, illegal exporting, or some big debt he owed her that kept him tied up.

One afternoon, I sat in the salon bar next to an open window, drinking warm soda, a slight breeze moving the hot air over my shoulders. It was a hot, humid afternoon, and no one was there except Begner. I sat alone, my internal chatter in full swing until I was pulled out of it when three women friends sat down next to me: Begner and Chino's sisters Columbia and Hilda.

"¡*Ola, Catalina!*" Columbia said. I looked up and greeted them.

"It's terrible what Milicho is doing, horrible!" Begner clucked indignantly while Columbia went to the bar for a bottle of Coke.

"He should be with you. *No lo entiendo.* I don't understand him," Columbia said sitting down next to me. She poured the warm soda into some glasses. I wondered if the women had any aguardiente to put in it. That was not something women did openly, only at night with their husbands.

"Well, *quién sabe*, who knows," I answered. "Perhaps he is serious about her, perhaps he loves her. *Quizás él la ama.*" I said this lightly, nonchalantly, as if it wasn't even about myself and Milicho.

"Want us to fix it for you?" Columbia asked. "*¿Quieres que te lo arreglemos?*"

"*¿Qué estás diciendo?* What are you talking about?" I was not always sure exactly what people were saying to me because of the holes in my Spanish. If I missed a key word or a slang expression, I sometimes got on a completely wrong track and ended up lost. I tried to be careful and make sure I understood.

"Maria. *La podemos arreglar para ti.* We can fix it for you," Hilda said with a slight smile.

I looked at her blankly.

"Don't you want Milicho back?" Begner asked.

"*Cierto,* of course!" I replied. I should not have been surprised that they had any knowledge or interest in my drama, given how little privacy I had in this place. Everyone knew what was going on, with me, with the whole town, and no one had any boundaries.

Boundaries, now that's a laugh, I thought. *That is about as foreign a concept here as a woman having a profession.*

But Begner was serious. Columbia chimed in.

"*Un mechón de su cabello,* get a lock of Maria's hair from her comb, and give it to us. We can fix it so Milicho won't want to be with her and will come back to you."

"Come on, *¡hable en serio!* I'm not going to do that. That's voodoo. Black magic, *un truco.* I know Milicho loves me but I'm certainly not going to trick him with that stuff!" I wanted him to come back to me on his own volition, not because of any spell.

"*Bueno,*" Columbia snorted, shooting back the rest of her Coke like a shot of whiskey. "*Piensas.* Think about it. We'll be around."

"*Como quieres.* Suit yourself," Begner said.

And with that, Begner returned to the bar and the other two left the salon. I considered it, for a moment, then let it pass. Ridiculous. *That couldn't possibly work, could it?* Another decision I came to regret.

I was crazy with missing Milicho. He and Maria left Atacames a few weeks later to live in Quito. No more waiting around for the occasional window break-in. I was desperate to find another love, to create a life without Milicho, and give me a reason to stay.

I did not have to wait long. My now-single status seemed to have been broadcast throughout the Atacames gossip network, the *chisme* newsletter, and soon Chino, one of the few unmarried and childless men, came sniffing at my door like the dog he was. I didn't mind the emotionally detached roll in the hay in between rolling joints and settled into a relationship with Chino, who offered company and sex and not much more. Sex was not a big deal with Chino, a little abrupt and meaningless, reminiscent of my pre-Milicho behavior in Berkeley and along the Gringo Trail. Chino would make a short stopover to jump on la gringita before heading out for a day of grifting and drinking.

With Chino it was a much calmer thing: we were not in love, we were friends, and there was little emotion between us. We were the same age, and he was confident, smart, sexy as hell and just as wicked. Tall and thin, the blackest of his clan, with kinky hair, he could easily fit in with the young men in East Los Angeles. He seemed to always be up to something, dealing along the edges of truth. He made his living by doing scams, *negocios* of some sort or another, selling pot to the tourists, running fish, anything to make some plata. He partnered with his sister Leonore in a new comedor, but after the construction was finished, he did so little work she kicked him out. He loved to get high on trago like his father and pot like his brothers. A few years before, he and Milicho spent time in Guayaquil working as cooks and doing dope deals on the side.

I didn't love him, but maybe he was a way to get as close as I could to Milicho. I am sure Milicho knew Chino came by now and then, but he didn't seem to care, knowing Chino would never commit to me or anyone. Milicho could still have me as a default.

With Chino it was not lovemaking, and it was often cold. One night after a disappointing fuck, we talked about it.

"I need much more, more kissing and touching and going down."

"*No me gusta hacer esso,*" he said. He didn't like it so wouldn't do it. "*Lo siento.* Sorry. No." He was pretty clear about it.

I realized if I was going to be involved with a selfish man who made me feel ashamed of my vagina, I'd rather masturbate. I did not try to say this to Chino, why bother? He was not someone I could trust with my feelings, or with anything else for that matter. He knew where I stashed my money and even helped me bury the weed I brought to sell. One time he invited me to spend the evening with him and some friends from Quito who were partying on a boat. I spent the night on the boat, too dark and rainy to walk back to my casita, and in the morning, Chino was long gone. It turned out he went to my casita during the night and dug up the weed. He took my dope then wouldn't talk to me for three days because I asked him about it. I now knew all too well Chino's game; he was a fucker and not to be trusted.

There was always a slight aroma of deception in Atacames, an uneasy sense I got that people in the village were somehow skirting on the edges of honesty. It was partially caused by my incomplete understanding of what was going on around me. I was not fluent enough and missed the subtle nuances in conversations. Some locals eyed the tourists who came to Atacames from Quito or Europe as prey, as opportunities to make money. They also stole from each other frequently and openly. They took things with a sense of entitlement; if they liked something, they would try it on and wear it.

Certain things were meant to be shared, like food and dope and cigarettes, but here, anything people had was for all to use. One could say they were socialists, less concerned with the capitalist ethos of private property, perhaps a product of a culture of poverty. On the other hand, one could say they just liked to steal things.

I had the sense that these people did not trust me. I understood that. I was neither tourist nor local, neither staying forever nor passing through. I was living in a state of liminality, of ambiguity. I wanted nothing more than to be part of the community, chat with the women in the afternoons, drink trago and dance cumbia in the bar in the evenings, but I was not really a local and never would be.

CHAPTER 41:

LUCHO

After being in Atacames for a few more months, I still had not begun any projects or figured out what I needed to do to renew my tourist visa. I just hung out in the heat and sun and got high every day. I had become a member of a certain class of people —bohemians, hippies, artists of the soul, adventurers of a kind — committed to not being committed. Others would call us lost, or just goofing off. I kept thinking I needed some substantial involvement, exciting people doing exciting things, a situation where I didn't feel like I was only watching the movie I was playing in. I had become gossipy and what's worse, lazy. I needed incentive, a good kick in the ass.

Truth was, I was not going to find that incentive in Atacames. Creativity is a very lonely thing, and to get anything done, like playing guitar or writing or making art, meant hours alone in the house without company or distraction. But I liked kibbitzing around with the *gente*, getting out of my casita and hanging out in town. It was more fun now that I knew everyone so much better, especially the women, and I could understand the language more and more as time passed. There I was a different person, not so guarded, more in my emotions. I liked being La Catalina, freer, sexier, desired. Love and sex became my drug, my addiction, and without Milicho I was afraid of going through a painful withdrawal. So I turned toward another, Luis Enrique, or "Lucho" as he was called, hoping to replace the heart connection I had lost.

Ah, Lucho. Lucho was dangerous, intense, literate. He was smaller than Chino, with a slow, low voice, deep dark eyes, a tight muscular build, and an easy swagger. He was irresistible — professional and mature, sexy and educated — and I was doomed.

Lucho was the public health officer for the area and did not hang out that much during the weekdays. I only saw him in the evenings at the salon or playing football on the beach on the weekends.

One evening he sat down at my table at the salon.

"*Ay, Catalina,*" he said in his low, slow voice. "*¿Quieres un trago?*"

"*¡Si mon!*" I replied, smiling, always enjoying using local slang.

He poured a shot of aguardiente into my glass. We sat close for a while and when Begner turned up the cumbia record on the boombox, we danced, slow and close. It was intense and electric, as was the sex that happened later that evening. Our lovemaking was hot, with passionate words of connection and desire I knew were probably bullshit, but I was sucked into a vortex of need and possibility. *Maybe this could be real? Maybe he will take Milicho's place and give me a reason to stay?*

The problem was that I was scorned by my friends for getting involved with Lucho, as if I were cheating on Milicho. I was Milicho's girl. Forget the fact that he had left me for Maria. True, he insisted I wait for him, but I was losing hope. Milicho's family, his sisters especially, were furious with me when I started up with Lucho, for reasons far beyond their desire to see me be with their brother. I was sleeping with the enemy and didn't even know it.

I had stepped into some tropical version of the Montagues and the Capulets. Lucho's family were enemies of Milicho's family for years. I never found out what started the blood feud. It is hard to understand, in a village where everyone knows each other, sleeps with each other, has kids with each other, is related to each other and does business with each other. Here people are related by blood, by marriage or by sex.

Milicho's family became mine as soon as we started living together. His sisters were my *cuñadas*, sisters-in-law, and Señora Inez my suegra, my mother-in-law. Then for a while I was part of Chino's family. All his sisters called me cuñada and expected me to eat at their houses just as Milicho's family had expected me to eat at theirs. And then that faded as my sexual life with Chino faded as well.

Now Lucho's family — his father, Don Jacobo, and mother, Dona Esquila — would become mine. I could become the *nuera*, the daughter-in-law, simply by sleeping with their son. Usually the changeovers were loose, and nobody seemed to really care. The familial relations only lasted as long as the sexual relationship itself. If not, everyone in town would be calling everyone else cuñada. But in my case, turning towards Lucho while waiting fruitlessly for Milicho was a near-fatal mistake.

My affair with Lucho was powerful, passionate, insecure and volatile. Not like the sweetness and security and rightness of my time with Milicho. Being with Lucho felt like a fiery interlude that had no future, no honesty, consisting of late-night meetings and mysterious absences. Yet my desperate loneliness drew me to him and made me put up with it all.

My life had become a bad *telenovela*. I was playing a crazy game, sleeping with both Chino and Lucho while still hoping for Milicho to come back to me. One evening, after spending a few hours having sex in the afternoon, Lucho said goodbye because he needed to work in the morning out of town. I went to the salon, where Chino and I danced excitedly together before I went back to my casita. He came by a little while later, wanting sex.

"*Me gusta una mujer pila,*" he said as he tapped my forehead. He liked bright women. He said he believed I wanted him.

He was right, I did want him in that moment. I loved Chino in a way unique to him. Milicho was "my old lover," a very warm, friendly thing to have, but Chino was a friend who helped ease my loneliness. We had a nice fuck; I asked him not to sleep over and he left. Lucho came knocking early in the morning before his work, so I was glad I was alone. I had no idea what I was doing, and it was crazy, but it was also kind of fun.

A few weeks after my affair with Lucho began, Milicho came back to Atacames alone. We walked on the beach and the love flowed again. We made love in my casita, in our sweet and passionate style, like before. That evening in the salon we danced and drank and smoked. Milicho got quite drunk as we sat together in the salon and talked.

"*Te quería bastante.*" He said he had loved me a lot.

"*¿Y ahora?*"

"*También*, also."

I told him the truth, that I loved him still, too, and always would, but that we were with others right now, then I left the salon. Chino got up to come with me, but I told him no and went to my casita alone. Lucho came to my house later that night, and a few hours after that, Milicho stumbled in, still drunk, wanting to pick up where we left off. He went crazy when he saw Lucho in my bed.

"*¡Mala puta gringa!*" he shouted at me.

Lucho got up and walked out, leaving me with Milicho.

"You want to make love to me knowing you will leave again to be with Maria? *Estoy aquí in Atacames.* I am here and you are living in Quito with Maria!"

I was furious that he was mad at me for being with Lucho when he had someone else. He was angry and jealous and left me in pain. He drank the rest of the night and came back in the morning, crashing out on my bed. I wanted him to stay forever but he left a few hours later. He probably would not have minded finding Chino in my bed, but Lucho? That was unacceptable. It was ok for his ex to sleep with his pal but not with Lucho, who was not his pal.

Besides, I seemed to be the only one in the chisme network who did not know at the time that Lucho was involved with a woman in Sua, the next town south, who was pregnant with his child. That circus night should have been a real laugh, and I knew someday I would think it was funny.

But really, I had become the town puta, it seemed, and my little casita a lone red-light district down a side street of the tropical beach town.

**

The next day, I realized I needed some space and decided to go to Quito with Jade before she left for Boston.

Jade had arrived in Atacames with her baby, tiny Chita, a few weeks before. She was the French woman who had gotten involved with Tarzan, Chino's older brother. Tarzan, whose real name I never knew, was quieter and sweeter than Chino, and more trustworthy. He got his nickname because of his wild youth, running around in the forest with his dog, knives hanging from his belt. He was very good with his hands, making furniture and building houses. Like Chino, he was a good cook, and like Chino and their father Don Rogelio, he loved to drink.

Tarzan had a strong jealous temper, despite his quiet demeanor, and he and Jade had a lot of knock-down, drag-out fights. Even so, they stayed together for several months, and when she got pregnant, she decided to go to the States to have the baby.

She did a stupid thing and agreed to be a mule and ate some baggies of cocaine to make some money. The plan was for her to poop them out and get paid by the dealers once she got to Boston. The plan fell through when the baggies broke open in her system and she almost lost the baby.

Chita survived, as did Jade, miraculously. And now they were back in Ecuador, but only for a while. Jade was leaving for Boston, since she had an expired visa and did not want to risk being deported. She did not want to leave but Tarzan refused to get married, and for Jade to marry someone else just for a visa seemed a little risky, even for her.

When we were leaving for Esmeraldas on the way to Quito, Milicho decided to go, too.

"You're traveling with Milicho?" Señora Margarita said when she saw us get into the *camioneta,* the van that would take us to Esmeraldas to catch the bus to Quito.

"*Mas o menos.*" More or less.

I am sure the women were all wondering if Milicho and I were together again, and so was I. We talked and kissed in the camioneta and walked close in Esmeraldas. For one night on the bus, we were together, *como antes,* just like before. We kissed and fooled around and slept in each other's arms all the way to Quito.

"*¿Cuando haremos amor?*" he said, asking when we would make love.

"*En Quito,*" I said.

"*¿Dónde?*"

"*Vamos a un pensión.*" I dreamed of getting a room and really being together. But when daylight hit and Quito was real, the dream faded again, and he went off to Tumbaco where Maria was waiting. I felt sad and confused and overwhelmed with love for him.

I told Jade, "I love him, that's still true. There is still so much love between us, but he is not going to leave Maria. I am going to try to love Lucho the best I can."

I thought about Ellen and Sara and how it had been when we were in Quito the first time. Now, *después de un año y medio*, a year and a half later, how things had changed, how I had changed, and how different Quito was to me. Quito made me sad now, thinking of Milicho. I went into a hippie shop called Hojas de Hierba, Leaves of Grass, where Esther, the bilingual shop owner I had met before, chatted with me about my life.

"If you are not in need of money, why dissipate your energy on cookies and crap? Why not concentrate on your art? Why not take a sketch pad and pencil to the beach and do a little drawing?"

"You are right, but I can't seem to get motivated. I've been thinking about doing some batik, but it seems so difficult to get together and do on the beach. But I will try my best." I did a lot of batik in Berkeley, but it was in an art studio, with plumbing and a gas stove to heat the wax and space to hang the panels. I knew Atacames would be a difficult place to do it. It was a crazy idea.

It was interesting to be in Quito, a place I now seemed to know so well. There was Quito Sur, a colonial town with cobblestones and iron gratings and small tiendas, *picanterías*, street vendors and open markets. There was the Avenida Amazonas filled with boutiques and hotels, outside cafés, gringo tourists, BMWs and taxis, *heladerías* and beggars, and Quito Norte, a sprawling urban mass of ugly concrete houses and huge apartments, factories, airports and middle-class people.

I was so used to Quito I sometimes forgot what I was looking at: Indios with bare feet and bundles walking beside spiffed-up *flacos*, young students just out of school. In the buses there was every person and accent imaginable, from the very poor to the very rich, some with suits, others with ponchos and Latin faces; some in blue jeans, others in indigenous dress, high heeled shoes or no shoes at all. Quito was all mixed up and always interesting.

Back in Atacames, after putting in my application for a visa renewal, I started up my cookie business again and made a whopping profit of 80 sucres, about five bucks. It was definitely not a viable business plan, so I shut it down. I then got everything for the batik project and had a great time buying all the supplies, because the shopkeepers in Esmeraldas understood me. I needed to build a worktable and get some pots and do a lot of experimenting with the dyes. I was into it and glad to be excited about something. The muchachos, Chino, Tarzan, and the other cousins, went only so far to help me. They were still spending most of their time drinking in the salon or hanging out in the plaza. It was a good lesson to learn, that when it comes right down to it, no one may be there when help is really needed.

Jade came back from Quito, having decided not to go to Boston, and moved in with Tarzan and Chita. She was desperately looking for a way to fix her visa so she would not be deported. It was nice to have someone to talk to in English, another foreigner, another woman trying to exist in this place, and Jade and I spent time together when we could, but she was home most days with Chita.

"Why have I chosen such an un-feminist situation to live in?" I sighed. "The people I hang out with, except for passing gringas, are men. I am usually the only woman in the gang. It's getting better with you here and I'm getting to know Leonore and the other sisters better."

"I know what you mean," she replied. "I came back here to be with Tarzan, to make a family, but he is never here."

"I am really alone a lot, like you are," I said. "And the strange thing is I've chosen to be here, to struggle against the not-so-subtle demon of sexism. But I feel good here. I like the attention, the specialness, standing out in the crowd."

"It's insidious, really, wanting the attention and getting treated badly at the same time," she agreed. Jade picked Chita up from the crib and jiggled her on her knee. "I will have to leave at some point. Probably soon, for Chita's sake."

"I tell you, Atacames is the land of the lotus eaters." I picked up a joint and took a hit, blowing the smoke out the window away from the baby. "All I do is pass my days pleasurably, and I fear the eventual stagnation of my mind."

I told Jade about my life in Berkeley, how before my travels I was so involved with graphic art and batik, along with playing piano and political activism.

"It's becoming clear that for my own good I cannot dream of staying here for very long. Even though in another year I could possibly get a teaching job or something," I mused.

"Another year? I couldn't do it. Besides, they will never give us that long of a visa."

Jade was right. After months, my visa still had not been approved.

"Such assholes in this bureaucracy, and so inefficient it's a wonder the country progresses at all," I grumbled. "In another month I will have to leave the country for another visa. What a game."

The batik idea was, as I feared, impossible to do there. I needed more space, more equipment, better dyes, a studio. My kitchen could not suffice for both a kitchen and art studio. I had to scratch that idea and hope to be hired to teach English to the elementary kids, my only hope of pulling out of the doldrums. If I couldn't get my visa renewed, I would have to leave for six months and come back.

Or not.

But I loved Atacames, my house, my friends. My life with the people kept expanding, my language flowering into slang.

Milicho and Maria came back again from Quito and were living in the casita next door again, but I rarely saw them. I spent time with Lucho now and then, when he wasn't working or gone somewhere. Our sex was hot, and his words were charming and romantic, but I did not love him, not yet at least, and I remained on guard.

CHAPTER 42:

MEASLES

I spent the next few weeks going around with Lucho into the countryside with a group of missionary volunteers from Amigos de Latin America, a Mormon charity organization, in Ecuador for a vaccination expedition. I was asked to be the translator, helping two young blond Mormon men from Utah administer TB vaccinations to screaming children. We went all around Atacames, and then to Salima, Playa Grande, and other villages deep in the campo, a few days' walk from Atacames.

We gave shots in the schoolhouses, slept on the floors of churches and schools, and tramped around in mud up to our knees. The days spent doing vaccinations offered a new perspective about the way the people lived in such a poor country to the two blue-eyed, oblivious American do-gooders, who tried not to see any of it.

The land was gorgeous, the countryside thick with trees of a hundred shades of green: guavas, *toronjas*, papaya, and mangos seemingly falling from the sky. The people were so courteous and hospitable, country folk of a special kind. The last village we went to, Cumba, was celebrating the Fiesta del Carmen, so we stayed overnight and all the next day before returning to Atacames.

The next night after we got back, Lucho came in with a sad expression.

"*No quiero quedar in Atacames.*" He told me he didn't want to stay in Atacames, that he was putting in for a transfer, partly because of his dissatisfaction with working in Atacames and partly because of me. "*Necessito un poco distancia, para pensar.*"

I was not too sure what was going on, or why he needed distance from me.

"*Te quiero mas ahora, mas fuerte.*" He said he loved me more now. I wanted to believe that he was indeed falling harder for me, but I had my doubts. He told me he was unsure of my feelings for him.

I guess he was right; I was not sure of anything, and I was still keeping my guard up. Plus, I was a liar. I was with Chino occasionally, and I still loved Milicho.

"*Quiero estar contigo,*" I told him. "I want to be with you, but I want to stay in Atacames."

The director of the school had said I could work there two or three hours a week in the sixth grade, and I could teach a night class in the village and possibly a class in Esmeraldas. The jobs would give me a visa that would allow me to stay in Atacames.

And now he wanted to leave.

After Lucho left the casita, I lay awake in the hammock for a long while, going over everything in my head.

Now I don't know anything anymore. Living here is still some kind of weird romantic fantasy that I can't and won't pull myself out of. Maybe it would be better to split, but where do I go and to what?

The year was just gliding along like a riptide pulling me out to sea. I could not catch hold and get control, and whatever creative energy I still had was draining away month by month. I got up from the hammock to go to sleep.

All I know is I'm stuck in this place, with these people. I don't know if it's bad for me or good for me, but whatever it is, I love it here.

About a week after we returned to Atacames, I had a low-grade fever and generally felt like shit. It was a glorious day, but I could not even stand up, let alone swim. I stumbled back from the beach to my casita and promptly fell down, broke my eyeglasses, and became hysterical. I sent word to Lucho to come and waited all day, crying and feverish.

Finally, I went to the salon, and there he was playing cards. I asked Lucho to come outside and talk, and in the middle of the street I broke down and cried. He stayed sitting at the table, not looking up, with no intention of getting up. I leaned against the doorway for a moment, too shaky to stand, then staggered back to my casita and crawled into my hammock for the night. He showed up in the morning, figuring to find Milicho or Chino there. No one was there but me lying in the hammock, still with a fever.

"*Nunca me hables así,*" he scolded. "Don't reprimand me in the middle of the street so the whole town knows our business."

He was right, I guess. I should have had more discretion, but I was too upset and too sick to care.

The next day I fell into delirium. I'd had chicken pox as a baby, but never measles, and unbeknownst to me, there had been a measles epidemic in the campo where I'd been helping vaccinate kids against TB. I was quarantined in my house and even the visiting doctor would not come to help, fearing his four-year-old son would be exposed to the disease.

Here I was, almost twenty-five years old, living in a small bamboo house on stilts with no running water, no toilet, a mattress on the floor and a hammock as my couch. I lay in the hammock for a few days, I don't know how many, in fevered delirium. I ate nothing, drank water, and somehow managed to pee into a coconut bowl and crawl to the door to empty it outside. I don't remember much more than that, except for the feeling that I was dying.

No one came to help or even see if I was alive. No one. Not Milicho, not Lucho, not Chino, not their sisters, not the village doctor.

I could not help but think it was all my fault. I was caught in the middle because of my stupidity, loving three men, loving too much, playing around with sex too much. And because of my transgressions, I was left to die in my hammock alone.

I woke now and then in the day's heat, too worn out to brush away the flies on my face. Mosquitoes attacked at dusk, and the air sat on me wet and heavy. I couldn't even swing the hammock enough to make a breeze.

So this is what dying feels like, I thought. *Am I dreaming or am I awake? Maybe they'll come. Chino or Clodo, los muchachos, they must know I am here. They will come soon.*

No one came and the day passed. I was so hot, an internal heat that would not subside. *At least I am not getting cold. If I were cold, I would be dead.* The waves of flushed and burning skin gave me odd comfort, letting me know at least I was alive.

There was someone at the door, finally. I couldn't see; I was practically blind without my eyeglasses. I couldn't call out, my voice powerless. The door to my house opened slightly and a hand pushed a bowl onto the floor. The house was high up from the ground on stilts, so I could not see the person, only the hand, but I knew who it was. The hand was old, fingers gnarled. The bowl, a half coconut shell, was filled with a milky liquid-like rice water.

"*Toma.* Drink this," Señora Inez said, and she pulled the door closed.

I dropped out of the hammock and crawled on the floor to the bowl. I drank the cool brew slowly, my head over the bowl like a cat. Then I fell asleep where I lay on the floor, my body curled around the bowl.

Señora Inez came the next day and pushed another bowl through the door. She came again a third day. I saw nothing else, only her hand pushing the bowl through the door.

The next day my fever broke, and spots appeared on my face and body. I could open my eyes and sit up on my mattress. I don't know what was in that brew, perhaps some ancient African healing magic, but I suspect it had a large dose of love.

Maybe it was only rice water, not medicine, but whatever was in that brew made me see and hear what I had not been paying attention to. Maybe it had nothing to do with curing measles; maybe the fever had run its course by itself, but when I awoke from the delirium I awoke to the truth, that I was not cared for or cared about by the men I thought loved me, and it was killing me. For the second time, Señora Inez was the one who was there to heal me.

Eventually my strength returned. I could not go outside, though, as I was still under quarantine, and still had to pee in a bowl and push it outside. Slowly I was able to eat, speak, talk, and drink, and my life came back. Someone brought me more water and food — I could not see who — but I assumed it was Señora Inez. Soon Clodo showed up, then Chino as well, but not Milicho or Lucho or their sisters.

I got well with no scars, no loss of hearing, no more fever. When I was finally strong enough to walk outside and was no longer quarantined, I went to see Lucho at the salon and asked him to come to my casita.

"*Después un rato,*" he retorted, in a bit, and turned away. At which point I said, "If you don't come now, don't come again." And he didn't.

Three days of hell and tears later, I went to his house. We made love but he was cold, so cold, so insensitive, utterly different. I asked him if he wanted to continue with me and he said no. It seems he just fell out of love as quickly as he fell in. He was drunk, yet not that drunk to say something he did not mean.

It was a matter of pride, for both Lucho and me. I was hurt and gave an ultimatum. He was offended and pissed at being handed that ultimatum. He had told me about Gloria, the woman in Sua who had his child. He was coming from a breakup with her and did not feel like being called on his shit anymore. I did not think about or consider that he had a child, and I believed him when he said his relationship with her was over. But now things had played themselves out. Lucho was no longer in my life. He left me in his house in the middle of the night.

In the *madrugada*, a lovely sad dawn, I dressed and went across the footbridge to the beach. I sat on the sand for a long time going over everything that had happened, and I finally decided it was time to leave for good. I had had one painful experience of lost love. I loved Milicho more than anyone in my life, yet I left him and lost him. I was trying to somehow regain that feeling of security and love with someone else, but it didn't happen. If the one thing I depended on to fulfill me, to stimulate me, to give me a reason to stay — if that one thing proved to be as superficial and unreliable as it appeared — then what did I really have? Whatever I had, and whatever I thought I could create, was gone.

I thought about the other disappointing love affair with Chino, for me a masochistic problem. He was purely an opportunist when it came to sex, and he used my attraction for him and my horniness, without giving me any love. He would come when he knew Lucho could not. And I, like a fool, sometimes gave in and other times threw him out. But he played well on my vulnerability. He told lies about things I supposedly said, whether out of jealousy, hurt pride, or pure evil, I will never know.

But I was sure he was instrumental in turning Lucho away from me. The one man in Atacames I could truly trust and whom I loved sincerely I could not have. Milicho was still with Maria, despite his months of promises and requests that I wait for him.

"*Esperate*, wait just a little bit longer," he said again and again.

The women had told me months ago to just get a lock of Maria's hair, and they would fix it so Milicho would love only me. I refused. I wanted him to come to me fair and square, no black magic. I knew the spells never lasted.

So here I was, months later, not with Milicho, dumped by Lucho, banished from my English teaching job because of the measles quarantine, too tired to think of another way to renew my visa, and too depleted and hurt to stay.

CHAPTER 43:

YOU DON'T DROWN BY FALLING IN THE WATER. YOU DROWN BY STAYING THERE.

Atacames seemed like a calm sea: It appeared so safe and comfortable yet still had a current that pulled me down. It is like any strange ocean I enter. Sometimes the sea seems clean and safe, without fish or seaweed or trash or creatures that can harm me. The currents seem mild, the waves small and insignificant, hiding the riptides underneath. Tourists don't face those risks; they generally float above the tides, passing through without attempting to dig deep or dive down. They don't stay that long, often don't speak or understand the language, and stay in the comfort zone of other tourists.

At times I felt I was at risk of drowning, of losing my bearings. I did not know enough about who the people were to find a safe place with them. I was made the fool by my incomplete comprehension of the world I was swimming in, and I could not push myself out of the currents. I knew then I had to leave so I wouldn't drown.

A few days after Lucho left me in his house, I went over the bridge to Señora Inez's casita. We sat at the wooden table as she poured me a cup of coffee.

"*Debes quedarte y casarte con Milicho.*" Señora Inez was insistent. She said she would make Milicho leave Maria, that he was supposed to be with me, and I was supposed to be in Atacames. "*No te vayas.*"

"But I have no more life here," I said with sadness in my voice. *What is there for me at home, though?* I thought silently.

Later that afternoon, I sat at one of the beach palapas where the travelers hung out, having a drink with a gringo who had been on the road for a very long time and was ready to go back to Cincinnati. I talked to him about my sadness about leaving.

"Well, you can't stay here forever doing nothing, smoking dope, getting stupid, living with a bunch of illiterate fishermen."

He had been in Atacames for just a few days. What did he know of the magic of the place? But there was truth to what he said. Later I met up with Clodo at Señora Marguerita's comedor down the beach. We sat down for a meal of fried corvina, rice and black beans.

"This is paraiso," he said. "The most beautiful place on earth. Why would you want to leave? Stay here, have babies, just live your life. Why do you spend so much time worrying and thinking so hard? You are here now, so let's get high and go to the river."

I had to laugh. He was right, but so was the gringo from Cincinnati. I was in a soft trap of my own making. Atacames was a luxury, a life of play and enjoyment, my intellectual life a distant memory. Since coming back to Atacames, I tried to find that niche I had with Milicho, but it was different. I had fun, I danced a lot, and I fell in love all over again. But this time I fell in love with the prospects of a future here. I was looking for that reason to stay, unlike the one-day-at-a-time attitude I had with Milicho. I forgot my distance, forgot the movie, and played my role in it too seriously.

Whatever was waiting for me had to be faced, because I no longer had love to look forward to and be excited about. I felt as alone and detached as when I came, yet still with as much love for the place as ever. I often wonder if I had just hung in there through that desolate day on the beach, lost in broken promises and a broken heart, and stayed, what my life would be like now. There is no way to know.

I got together with Lucho a few times, just to talk. After my freak-out, things cooled. I made it clear that I was leaving, that I didn't want to try at it any more than he did.

"Come back in a year's time to Atacames. And I will be waiting for you. Will you come? *Si o no?*"

"*Es imposible a saber*," I replied. "And why would you wait a year for me but not want to be with me now?"

"*No puedo ahora.*" He could not freely be with me now; his relationship with Gloria was not over and his life was in shambles, or so he felt. I wanted to leave him with our love affair, such as it was, complete. Any promise to meet him next year would leave us with some romantic fantasy that our relationship was intact and undamaged, and that was not true.

"*Ya me voy*," I told him, "*y no surfriré mucho.*" I told him I would not suffer much and neither would he.

For my part, I'd lived a wonderful, ego-fulfilled, sex-filled year there, of this I made no pretense. I drenched myself in passion and emotion, and I saw where it could lead, to all the tears and pleas and games one plays in a romance. I knew that when I had another relationship with a man, it had to be different; it had to be true. I knew damn well when I used the word love with Lucho, I never fully believed it.

But with Milicho there was a good, full relationship and I can truthfully say I loved him then and love him still.

**

A few days later, it was August 12th, my birthday. I had not really celebrated it the year before, but this year I was turning twenty-five. It felt significant, the peak of my twenties. I felt the wonderfulness, the fullness of twenty-five, a time of adventure, of going for it, of seeing it all. I told people about my birthday and invited them to my casita for a party.

We had a sweet gathering, and it felt like a going-away party as well as a birthday celebration. Eduardo came in from Esmeraldas bringing some wine, and Napo and David, two musicians who traveled around Ecuador, were in town and brought guitars. They sang boleros, and they joined in when I played and sang Beatles songs. Clodo and Chino showed up, along with Jade and Tarzan, Cabeza Loca, Begner and Columbia. Neither Lucho nor Milicho were there, a bittersweet reminder of how my life had changed. I had decided to stay through the Fiesta de Atacames, which started on August 30th, a fitting way to complete my life there.

A few days later, I saw Lucho in the salon. It was his daughter Chilina's birthday party. Everyone was sitting at a long table, but Lucho gave no sign of *saluda*, nor said anything to me. Even though I wanted it to be over, it still was a punch to the gut to be rejected like that.

I'd like to analyze myself sometime, figure out why a nice healthy feminist like me does such fucked-up bits with men? Maybe I've spent this year stuffing myself with masochistic doses of sexist behavior to get it all out of my system, I laughed to myself. I was spending a lot more time writing in my diary, lying in bed with my early morning dreams. That last episode with Lucho left me astounded. *Ya basta. I've had enough.* I was disengaging little by little as the time to leave got closer.

By the third week of August, everyone was getting hyped up for the festival. People were busy painting houses and papering walls. Their interior decorating was amazingly simple: They put butcher paper, newspapers or magazine pages over the bamboo walls and painted on the paper. The locals focused on choosing festival queens and getting new clothes made. Lucho painted his house, both he and Chino got new shoes, and Columbia was busy making new *vestidos*, fancy outfits, for her kids. More and more restaurants, jugo stands, bars and comedors sprung up.

People were looking forward to making some money from the tourists who came for the festival, enough to get them through the rainy season, enough to buy a tape player or new canoe.

CHAPTER 44:

THE VULTURES

A few days before the festival, Columbia and Marguerita, another woman friend, came to check out my house for stuff I might be giving away. They were in the casita when I came back from the beach.

I stood outside the doorway listening to the two women and watching them through the slats in the walls and thought of that scene in *Zorba the Greek* when the old women, all dressed in black, circled around the bed of the dying woman like vultures, waiting to swoop down and steal all the belongings from the house. The only difference was that I wasn't dead yet, and these women weren't waiting for my corpse to get cold. I hadn't even left yet and already the women were picking through my things and taking whatever they wanted.

"*¿Sabes qué?* I knew it was La Catalina who killed those puppies. I knew it, *ella tiene mal ojo.* It had to be her. You know how she kept looking at those puppies — *demasiado fuerte* — too strongly, with too much *mal ojo*. And they were all dead the next day!" Marguerita kept mumbling about *mal ojo*, evil eye, and those puppies, as she sorted through my belongings. Why she remembered that from so many months before was unnerving.

"*No sabes con certeza*. You don't know that for certain," Columbia responded. "After all, it could have been worms, and Señora Inez would have said something if La Catalina was the one. *Y todavía* she still wants her to be with Milicho!" Columbia and Marguerita continued their chat as they put the things they wanted in a pile on the wooden floor next to the door.

"I don't know, I never trusted her. What was she doing here anyway? *Ella es rica*. Why did she want to live here? Look, she even puts her mattress on the floor. No bed!" Marguerita clucked as she picked through t-shirts and shorts and tried on sandals.

"*No lo sé*, I don't know, she always was nice to me and polite. She just asked too many questions." Columbia sat down in the hammock to rest for a bit.

"*¡Apúrate*, hurry!" whispered Marguerita. "She should be back pretty soon."

"*No te preocupes*. Don't worry," Columbia said, the hammock gently swaying as she spoke. "Catalina said we could have her clothes if we needed them. She is going home to *Los Estados*. She can buy anything she wants there."

I could see Marguerita fingering the strands of puka shells on the wood shelf above the suitcase.

"I think Milicho made this necklace for her. I better not take them. Besides, I can get them here for free. It's her money and her good things I want, not these silly puka shells. That's what Milicho and the other muchachos spend their time on, *no trabajan*, they don't do real work. That gringa got him away from doing what he was supposed to do. *Ella tiene la culpa*, it's her fault *los muchachos* don't work."

"*No seas tonta*, don't be silly. Do you really think she had that much power?" Columbia got out of the hammock and began to stuff clothes into a bag.

"*Tiene plata*. She has money," Marguerita snorted. "That is enough power, *no olvides*, don't you forget that!"

I guess that's all they think I'm good for, I thought, as I listened from outside the door. *All they care about is my stuff, my money, what I am going to give them, what they can take from me. No matter how long I live here, no matter how much I love them, I will never be anything but a rich gringa.*

CHAPTER 45:

FIESTA DE ATACAMES

Jade was leaving the same time I was, right after the festival.

"I wonder what they really think of us. I don't think they like me," Jade said as she was packing her things and getting ready to take baby Chita back to the States. I sat on a bench in the casita she shared with Tarzan, watching her fold the baby's clothes.

"A good question," I replied. "I know I am liked, but my image here may not always be the best. To some I'm just a hippie fucking a lot of men, which isn't far from the truth. But I am treated well, missed when I am gone, noticed when I return, and everyone greets me with one of my many names. It's quite comical, really. Poncho the Panadero calls me *Cata*, the bridge store lady calls me *Catuchka*, and Don Rogelio calls me *Catita*. The kids call me *La Galletera*, and everyone else calls me *La Catalina*. It could drive one nuts, but it makes me feel accepted, maybe even loved, even if I'm not."

Jade laughed. "Maybe I should give you some more nicknames, some French ones, to add to the list!"

"I know they like me, but sometimes I think my behavior offends them," I said. "It's subtle, like glances and head tilts as I pass by. I do things that women here don't do, like swim in the ocean, wear a bathing suit, hang out with the muchachos, and smoke pot. This would be acceptable if I were a tourist passing through, but I am living here."

Jade picked the baby up and sat her down on her lap. "I felt it too, but in some ways my having a baby made me more accepted, perhaps. Here no one judges if you have a baby and you are not married. Everyone is upset that I'm leaving, though. But it isn't the healthiest place to raise a child."

"What do you think you will do when you leave here?" I asked Jade, whom I didn't really know that well. I knew she was French and had lived in the States for a while.

"I don't think I will come back here, not anytime soon. I need to set up a life for Chita, figure out some way to earn a living, keep her safe and healthy. Not do something stupid again like bring in cocaine! What about you?"

"I don't know when or if I will come back here. I love the whole strange silly scene, but I've been stuck in one place too long. Maybe I'll go to Boston and visit you. I could go to New York, where my brother lives, and get a job. Maybe I'll take the law school boards again. I took them before I left and tanked them. I would need to take it more seriously this time. I can tell you some of the things that I want to do, *por uno*, keep studying Spanish, keep using it. I want to learn photography and get a good camera, maybe get back into art."

"I didn't realize you were on the law school track. I thought you were just a hippie!"

We both laughed at that as Jade finished packing up her things and went

off to give Chita a bath.

"I won't be going to the festival that much, what with the baby. It will be too crazy."

"I'll see you afterwards, when it is time to leave."

I left Jade's casita and walked across the footbridge to the beach, a path that had become so familiar. I knew every house, every marker, the point on the beach where the sand got wider, the broken step at the end of the footbridge, the different shortcuts to my house to avoid the aggressive dogs, the path to the jugo shop. I knew when the cold sodas would be available at the small tienda in the morning, when the water truck came from Esmeraldas, when the sand became too hot to cross the beach. Atacames was my neighborhood, my home.

The night before the big blowout, I went to the salon to hang out with some of the women. Two Quiteñas, young women from Quito, sat at another table, with Lucho and Chino flying around them like moths.

One of the women, the one Lucho spent time with on the beach while I was crying over measles and my broken heart, was wearing the puka necklace I gave to him. Such nerve, to have her wear that in front of me. Somehow the necklace came up in conversation.

I answered Elda, "No, it's not Chino's necklace that Lucho gave to his novia, it's the one I gave Lucho, the son of a bitch." And we all agreed — Leonore, Columbia, Elda and me — that he was a real *hijo de puta.*

Leonore said, "Don't let him see you pissed. *A ellos les gusta verte enojarse.* They like to see you get angry."

"Nothing he can do now will affect me." I said it but it was not true. It affected me deeply.

When August 30th arrived, the whole town of Atacames became a party. There were bamboo dance floors set up along the beach and in the town. The beach bars blasted cumbia and salsa from their boom boxes, and the salon was at capacity. Hundreds of students from Quito and locals from neighboring towns swarmed in, cars lining the plaza and along the road from Esmeraldas, and aguardiente and beer flowed everywhere.

I partied with Chino and Clodo and so many other friends, but the fiesta passed without seeing Lucho at all. He told me later that he had had a big fight with Gloria. She searched his room and read all the letters he received from women, including one I wrote, and left them in shreds on his bed. She wanted to come back to him, and he did not want her.

**

I was in Atacames for the fiesta the year before, but it was so different. I was different. I had been in Atacames for six months by then, in love with Milicho and learning how to live there and live with him. I was shy, and I remember walking through the festival holding on to his hand for dear life. I did not party that much and there were no all-night bacchanals for me.

This year the fiesta was a whole other experience. It was as if I was a completely different person, as if I had broken out of myself. I danced like never before for three nights and came home after 6:00 a.m., slept not at all, drank whisky and smoked dope. I danced with all the passion and joy I had for this place. I danced out the heartbreak and sadness I felt about leaving. I danced for all the memories I would take with me. I danced to be alive.

I don't remember dancing when I was a child. I don't remember moving my hips with sensual abandon. Of course not. I was a chubby ten-year-old girl hiding under ugly plaid jumpers. I did not live in my hips or in my body. In high school my body was in hiding, too uncomfortable and embarrassed to show up. I listened to records, played piano and guitar and sang. I drank in the music through my fingers, the rhythms internalized, never showing on the outside. My body did not move to the music. I tried not to have a body; I tried to be invisible.

Then I was an eighteen-year-old virgin hiding under baggy overalls. I was not one of those hippie-haired, flowy-skirted girls swaying to the Grateful Dead or freeform jumping to loud Stones music in a high school gym or a friend's pool party. I didn't go to pool parties or dances. My body stayed home out of sight.

In my college days, there were rock concerts in the parks, banjo and fiddle festivals in Topanga Canyon, stoner jam sessions in friends' living rooms. I reveled in them, immersed in the music, but my body remained contained in dark, baggy clothing, along the back wall away from the dance floor or sitting in a group playing my guitar. I wore no jangling bracelets or bright colors, no V-shaped necklines or tightfitting tops, no lipstick or eyeliner, tight jeans or floppy felt hats.

Sure, there were moments of exploration, of pushing out from behind the curtain. I skinny-dipped in the lake at the hippie commune I lived in for a few months, high on mushrooms. I went braless, but never topless, my breasts safely nesting behind denim overalls and leotard tops. I was naked occasionally in bed with a man, the only time I did not feel fat. My weight was my burden and my shield, a decision I made at twelve years old, when I was at my heaviest, that my body was not to be revealed to avoid shame and embarrassment, not to be on display and certainly not to shake, rattle and roll in public. My body lived in silence, while my mind, my fingers, my talent, my music, my drawings, and my words lived out loud.

This was how I was raised, in a family of fat, brilliant women weighed down by judgment and body shame. My mother loved Broadway musicals and the American Songbook, even though she could not sing a note. She would rasp along with the records, smiling as she mouthed the phrases of "Someone to Watch Over Me." My big brother loved rock and roll, and my father loved to play guitar and sing songs of Roger Williams and The Weavers. But none of them danced and the music did not live in their bodies, either. My parents did not go dancing. Ever. I never saw them embrace, except in sorrow and consolation when someone died.

When I left home and wandered, I began to let go of the heavy outer trappings of who I was as I journeyed down the Gringo Trail, through the cities, the dry landscapes, the cold Sierra Nevada and Andes, down to lush green jungles and tropical beaches. As I traveled, I stripped off the heavy hiking boots and wool ponchos, oversized jeans and bulky sweatshirts. As I shed my clothing, I shed the weight of my embarrassment.

In Atacames, a damp, hot, lush place, I wore flowing skirts and cut off t-shirts. I found myself in funky bars letting the tropical beat of Cuban salsa and Colombian cumbia perforate my skin and penetrate my hips. Slowly my body allowed itself to move, to sway, to gyrate, to swivel, to dance. My tongue wrapped around the smooth liquid shapes of tropical Spanish, dropping the harsh consonants and flat, wide-angled vowels of gringo English. My language softened, my dress softened, my skin softened, and my hips began to sway when I walked.

I learned to dance, and my body learned to live out loud. I wore puka shell necklaces and gauzy blouses. I lived as La Catalina, without a past, without parents or brothers or a college degree or a car. My intellectual life receded into the background so my body and my heart could take center stage.

Years later, I was often asked why I chose to live in such a simple, often uncomfortable and risky place. But it was not the girl I was raised to be who lived in that place. It was a different girl, La Catalina, the one who lived in her body, spoke with her hips, loved from her heart.

It was this girl I took home and kept tucked inside myself, like a cherished dress I once wore.

CHAPTER 46:

THE DESPEDIDA

Monday night after the fiesta was the *Baile de Barrio Arrecha*, a big dance in a nearby village. I had not seen Milicho at all during the festival, but he was at the Baile. He took my hand, and we danced for a while, then we left at 3:00 a.m., making passionate love in my casita before returning to the salon. It was our goodbye to each other, the last time I would feel his body, his skin, his love. I cried all the way through it and held on to him for a long time. It no longer hurt, not being with him, but I cried out of sadness. I cared about him and loved him deeply and still I could let him go.

After the fiesta, I spent three days of quiet reflection, seeing the beauty again, sitting on the beach, swimming in the gorgeous ocean water, soaking it up. I spent three sweet nights with Lucho. He told me about his feelings like never before.

"*Me siento mucho dolor.*" But even though he felt real pain about my leaving, he never asked me to stay. "*No es un buen momento,*" he said. It was not a good time, but he wanted me to come back. He promised to come to Quito before I left for the States. He promised he would write and that we would be together again.

"*No creo que vuelva.*" I told him I did not believe I would come back. I did not believe his promises. I cried real, painful tears when I left him, without remorse or guilt, just sadness at my having to leave this place for my own good. I had to let all these people go. Atacames was like a drug, and I had to put it down.

On my last day, I had a nice *despedida*, a farewell gathering in the salon, with a lot of honest final conversations with friends. Milicho gave me a tender quick hug when I was leaving the salon. There were no longer any feelings to hide. The games were over, and we hugged in front of everyone. I took with me my regrets and the image of Milicho in the ocean that last day he was truly mine, the day I first left for Los Angeles, a memory so beautiful yet so excruciatingly painful. Maybe the pain would subside eventually, but the memories would not.

After leaving Atacames, I spent a few days in Otavalo during another fiesta, drinking *herbitos* and dancing salsa in the street. When I got back to Quito, staying at the house of some friends, Lucho called me from Eduardo's office in Esmeraldas. He missed me, he said, and seemed glad to hear my voice, and I felt the same. How crazy was I?

I called my parents and told them I wanted to come back and asked if they would wire me funds for the flight. They were relieved and happy to do so. Then I met up with some friends from LA, and we traveled together to Misahuallí on the Río Napo, the Ecuadorian Amazon area where Ellen and Sara and I had been in what seemed like a lifetime ago. We got there on a Saturday night, the cumbia music playing like in Atacames, and I had the urge to go out and drink *con la gente*. I missed Atacames badly and I still had the urge to turn around and go back.

I spent the week in Cuenca after my friends left. It was a wonderful visit, including an affair with Marcel, the student I met in Atacames, satisfying my older woman fantasy. I met his friends and hung out on the street corner near Luis Cordero Park. I chatted with his sisters as they prepared the family's meal and sat next to Marcel at the dinner table with his family. His two aunts, dressed in black lace like old Castilian widows, stared sternly at me.

I addressed his mother and aunts formally and in my best Spanish, or so I thought, and complimented them on the meal. What I thought I said was that it was the most delicious meal I had eaten in a long time, but Marcel kicked me hard under the table and the black-widow aunts gasped. What I actually said was more along the lines of, "This was the best fucking food I've stuffed myself with in like, forever, no shit!" I realized later that the Spanish I learned in Atacames was filled with expletives, street slang and gutter language. Who knew?

After a week, I returned to Quito, hoping to meet up with Lucho before flying home. I stayed a few more days in Quito until the wired money arrived for my ticket, but Lucho never showed, which was just as well.

I was tired of Quito, tired of buses farting black fumes, tired of the inconveniences, the phones that did not work, the electricity that went out every day. I was fed up with being harassed on the street by horny men trying to speak English to me like I was an idiot. But there was so much I knew I would miss: the corner tiendas, the street vendors, the Indio women wrapped in colorful weavings. I knew I would miss Ecuador with its gorgeous campo, lush green jungles and beaches of the coast, the banana and papaya trees, and the chirimoya bush in my front yard. I knew I would miss my life there.

The month I spent traveling around the country after leaving Atacames was well spent. It felt like a slow goodbye to a place I knew would always be a part of me.

CHAPTER 47:

LEAVINGS

While I waited in Quito for the day of my flight, I still questioned my decision to leave. I had so many regrets about leaving Atacames the first time. What does it take to decide to turn away from a place you have lived, a place you think of as home? There are conscious deliberate leavings in life and there are ones that just happen, without thought or plan. There are leavings by default, from a lack of alternatives, or in reaction to a dead end. There are leavings with regret and sadness, permanence and never looking back. There are leavings with one's foot in the door, assurances of a return, made less intense or frightening by the refusal to say it is final, even if it turns out to be. There are leavings that are cavalier and easy, and others that are filled with ritual and ceremony.

I took off for college when I was eighteen to a school in Oregon. I never saw my childhood home again; my parents sold the house in Beverly Hills right after I left. I had no idea I would never be in my bedroom again, never see my doll collection — lost in the move — or my cat, given to a neighbor. When I lived in Berkeley, I never could imagine living anywhere else, and when I left, I had no idea I would never live there again. That is what is so mysterious about leaving a place. While I live in a place it becomes my sole reference point; I am enveloped by it, its boundaries become my world. And then I leave, and that world disappears, and I step into yet another one.

I left the States for Ecuador twice and left Ecuador for the States twice as well, and each one was a different kind of leaving. The first time Ellen and I took off for Latin America, we plunged into the unknown. We were excited to go on a trip we believed would be half a year or less. Our moms, though not that happy about it, showed no tears or resistance, unaware that we would be gone for so long or travel to such risky places.

When I left Atacames for Los Angeles the first time, it was no big deal; it was a foot-in-the-door kind of leaving. I was only going for a short time, not leaving for good. For Milicho, my cavalier attitude was a stab in the heart, because he did not believe I was coming back. The short time I was gone did not matter; it was the kind of leaving that changed everything. Had I known that the day I left would be the end of our being together, I would have taken my decision a bit more seriously, been more aware of how my leaving felt to him. Perhaps he would not have gone with Maria, and I would have come back to a life with him, with children, perhaps.

The second time I left Los Angeles for Ecuador, after three months, it was not so easy. I had more permanence in mind. I packed a suitcase, not a backpack. I brought a guitar and a new tape player. I was no longer a vagabond; I was going back for good. I was leaving my home and my parents for real. Was it worth leaving my mother, still recovering from cancer, the moment her life crashed down on her, the moment my father walked out of their marriage? Would I have left had I known the life I was returning to had already disappeared?

Now I was leaving Ecuador to go back to Los Angeles, to go back home, and it filled me with sadness. I had returned to Atacames believing I would live there forever, then one day, I packed up my suitcase and said goodbye to my life there for good.

CHAPTER 48:

WELCOME HOME

The journey back to LA was exhausting and long. I flew from Quito to Mexico City, with a few hours' layover wandering around the airport in a state of anxiety, sadness and fatigue. The shiny marble floors and metal railings made me feel cold and claustrophobic. Finally, we lined up to board, and a young, well-dressed Mexican man started chatting me up. I must have looked the perfect target, total hippie with frizzed-out hair and a backpack. I had already checked my suitcase, guitar, and sleeping bag, the one with the baggies of excellent weed sewn into the lining. I watched from the window as my belongings were loaded onto the conveyer to the plane.

He spoke English very well. "Where are you from? Where are you going? How long have you been in Mexico? Are you traveling alone?"

I was so completely fed up with being hassled by men, especially in Mexico, so done with having to navigate around the constant intrusions and sexist banter, that I tried to ignore him, but he continued.

Finally, I snapped. "What, do you work here or something? Stop asking me questions and leave me alone!"

"Well, as a matter of fact, I do work here." He showed me his badge from the Mexican drug enforcement police. "Step out of the line. Now!" He grabbed my arm and pulled me to the side.

"Why? What did I do? I'll miss my plane!"

I was ushered into the women's bathroom where a stocky, scowling uniformed policewoman demanded I take off my clothes to search me. I spoke to her in Spanish, explaining how my plane was boarding as I took off my clothes, finally getting down to my underwear. She was digging into my backpack when I heard my name over the airport speakers, calling for me to board. I was crying now.

"*¡Mira, no tengo nada! ¡No hay nada!*" I sobbed, flashing my underwear at her so she could see there was nothing in them. She stopped rifling through the pack and tossed it at me and told me I could go. I threw my clothes on and ran to the gate, flushed and freaked out.

There was an older American couple standing in front of me in the boarding corridor, dressed like they had just gotten off a cruise ship. I was so glad to be near them, feeling the comforts of home, and told them what had just happened. The man looked at me, a disheveled hippie with all the trappings of the counterculture and said, "I think they should line all the drug dealers up against the wall and shoot them."

I stared, without response. I was returning to Nixon's America. *Welcome home*, I said to myself.

When I had settled into my seat, thankfully far away from that man, I opened my pack to get a snack and unzipped the side pocket. In it was a baggie filled with seeds I was taking home as a gift to friends who liked to grow their own. "Holy shit!" I gasped quietly. If the policewoman had found that, I would be in prison for a long, long time. Unlike the muchachos, I couldn't bail myself out. Once again, I'd dodged a bullet, big time.

I'd always felt that there was an angel sitting on my shoulder when I traveled in Latin America, like there was some guy holding an umbrella over my head to protect me from getting hit with shit. It was the opposite of Joe Btfsplk in the *L'il Abner* cartoons, the jinxed guy who always had a cloud above his head, raining only on him. In all the adventures and stupid decisions and precarious locations I found myself, I stayed safe. My lovelorn heart may have been torn to shreds but I never got busted, jailed, raped, injured or deported.

The asshole policeman on the Colombia/Ecuador border was a close call, I admit. I had run-ins with Interpol, Mexican undercover drug cops, corrupt consular agents, run-of-the-mill thieves, and aggressively obnoxious men in dark streets and empty beaches. But my angel was always there, keeping me safe.

There were many times the odds were against me. Like the time Ellen and I were in a truck in the Andes that broke down and could have slid off the road down a thousand-foot cliff, but it didn't. It just stopped where it was and we, along with men and women sitting on corn bags and chewing coca leaves, spent the night on the floor of the truck bed and did not freeze to death.

Later, when I was wasting away from dysentery, then got measles with no clinic or medicine, I somehow survived unscathed. I could have become deaf, I could have died, but I didn't. My angel, perhaps in the guise of Señora Inez, was there so I could live to tell these tales.

**

I soon found myself at my mother's new condo near Century City, where she had moved after the end of her marriage. She had recovered from thyroid cancer, but her voice remained metallic and raspy, and it stopped her political and professional life. She had been very involved in the peace movements during the Vietnam War, an early member of Another Mother for Peace and Women Strike for Peace. She'd also had a thriving jewelry sales business for several years. She lost all that when she lost her voice.

Now in her mid-fifties, this was the first time in her life that she was on her own. She kept busy with discussion groups and bridge games, finding comfort in the company of other divorced and widowed women. She never remarried or even dated, and her health and happiness steadily declined over the next twenty-five years until her death at age seventy-nine.

She gave me the once-over when I arrived, not too happy with my disheveled appearance, but I could tell she was relieved I got home in one piece. I stayed in Los Angeles and stayed close to my mother until she died. My father remarried twice after the divorce, and moved farther away, first to Pasadena and San Fernando Valley, and later to Scottsdale, Arizona, where he lived until his death at age ninety-three. My parents remained good friends until the end, despite everything. I held on to my anger toward my father for a few years, but after a while I let it go, especially after my mother passed and I no longer had to navigate around her anger and sadness.

I spent the first few weeks home reconnecting with a few friends, mostly pals from high school, who still lived in LA. But I had been away for so long, first at Berkeley and then two years on the road, that I needed to create a new social life. Friends had changed, some got married and had kids, even my Berkeley friends had moved on. My closest friend in Berkeley was a radical feminist and very involved in socialist politics when I was there, but after I left, she moved to LA and married a wealthy doctor. When I came home, she showed up at my mother's house completely transformed, well-coiffed and bejeweled, in high heels and lipstick. I literally did not recognize her at first, the transformation was that shocking, and it was clear we would not be close again. I wondered if I had changed as much as she had, albeit in an entirely different direction.

I wanted to get busy and get involved in something creative. I took a photography course, got an article about life in Ecuador published in a women's magazine, and moved into a house in Ocean Park a few blocks from the ocean. I knew the only way I would be happy in Los Angeles was to get close to the beach.

It took a bit of adjustment to get used to living in Los Angeles after being gone so long, but I was a master of the freeways again in no time. It was, however, a bit unnerving to drive past a billboard with a ten-foot image of my brother Richard in scuba gear, advertising that film about a big fish.

A year after I returned home, I took off on a five-month trip through Mexico and Guatemala, this time with a new boyfriend, a sweet blond student from the Midwest. We were equipped with a Land Rover and camping gear. I was like a homing pigeon, drawn back to the Gringo Trail.

When we got back, we moved to Venice Beach, and I settled down. The boyfriend moved back to the Midwest and became a stockbroker. I joined the Los Angeles Women's Community Chorus, took life drawing classes at Art Center, and made new lifelong friends. I spent a few years working in cartoon animation before taking the LSATs again and applying to law school. My parents heaved a huge sigh of relief that my vagabond days seemed over.

When I first came back to LA, I dreamt crazily every night about Milicho and Atacames. I obsessed about Milicho, of seeing him again, of finding out if he truly loved me, and the fantasies of returning took a long time to fade. I wrote a long letter to Milicho, the only way I knew how to ease the pain of missing him. I never sent it but kept it and read it again years later.

Milicho my lover, even as I start this, I know it is difficult to write about you. It has been a year since we "broke up," a year since the day you spoke to me so coldly and told me you had another lover. And yet in the months that followed, living in the same village, seeing each other often, occasionally making love (but oh so occasionally), I never felt as if we had broken up for real. To this day I think of you as my lover, and when I think of Atacames, I think of you. I could not be with you, so I tried to love Lucho, but it was not the same. He was not a hippie. I never stopped loving you. And I still do.

CHAPTER 49:

ELIA

Ellen, in later years, took her Jewish name Elia. She'd returned to the States a few months before I did, but we did not know what paths our separate travels took until we reconnected a few years later.

She and Sara traveled to Argentina and Paraguay after leaving Bolivia but never made it to Colombia. After we separated in La Paz, our lives went off in different directions, yet we were impacted by the experiences on that journey in similar ways. I became an attorney representing indigent, mostly Black and Latino, clients, speaking Spanish and working in Latin American solidarity movements. Elia studied Spanish to fluency, traveled several times to Argentina and Mexico, worked as a paralegal in an El Salvadoran advocacy law group in San Francisco, and spent the rest of her life educating Latino immigrants in an Amherst, Massachusetts community college.

The conflicts we experienced during our travels together remained unresolved, however. We saw each other occasionally over the last decades at family gatherings, funerals for our grandparents and birthday parties for our fathers and mothers, yet we rarely wrote or called each other and never discussed our time together on the Gringo Trail. Elia suffered from constant gastrointestinal problems she'd developed during her travels. She survived uterine cancer only to die from intestinal cancer five years later. She was sixty-two.

A few weeks before she died, Elia told her sister to tell me that if I wanted to talk about anything from the past, if I had stuff to say to her, now was the time, since she knew she would be dead soon. When I heard that I said, "No, not really. It was a very long time ago and I barely remember who I was or what happened. Whatever broke us up was about those two young girls, not us now."

I did not tell her sister the truth. I did remember us then, but I did not want to go back there, back to who we were and how we were to each other. Elia was sardonic, judgmental and not light-hearted. She had fun, but with an edge. She would tilt her head to one side, squint one eye and slightly scowl, one hand on her hip. She did not hug much and held herself in tight. It was hard for me to get close to her, her wall of judgment too thick. She dated in high school, married young and ran away from it, then came out as a lesbian after our travels, living for a while in separatist lesbian communities. I was fat and rarely dated in high school or college, had sporadic short-lived sexual relations with men that rarely had substance, and felt unattractive and undesired.

For the months we traveled together, everywhere we went we were bothered by men, in the streets, in cafés, on buses, on trucks. They whooped and whistled and crooned, "*Ay, chicas, Ola, gringitas, guapas,*" making kissing noises and leering at us. Elia was annoyed; she sneered and never looked at them. I could not help it and sometimes looked up, my body language responding to the attention as I walked past, while she was ready to kick them in the groin. She got pissed at me often for my behavior, and there was a growing distance between us as the months went by.

I understood why she may have been angry with me for not being angry. Those men were disgusting, leering, intrusive, and presumptuous. I was a feminist from Berkeley, so why wasn't I outraged? My experiences in college with men and sex and relationships were not that positive or successful. No one had ever whistled at me before and I was attracted to the attention like a moth to a light bulb. To Elia, I suppose, I was a liar and a hypocrite. I remember feeling judged by her for years afterwards. But all that is probably my conjecture. In truth, what happened is that our lives just went separate ways. We never shared our stories or reminisced; we just drifted away from each other.

I went to see her a few days before she died, and we hugged and spoke to each other from the heart. Cancer softened her, dying softened her. I read her a few of my stories about our journey together and lay next to her on the day bed in her house in Northampton, a house I had never visited, filled with her life I did not know.

The last words I said to her were, "*Bien viaje.*"

"*Gracias,*" she said.

And then she went into palliative sedation that night and never woke up. She died a few days later.

CHAPTER 50:

THE RETURN: TWENTY YEARS LATER

In 1995, I spent a few weeks on a boat in the Galapagos with my brother Richard, his kids, and a film crew that was making a documentary with him. When the boat docked at Isla Santa Cruz for the day, I went to find Maga, an Atacamanian who I'd heard owned a clothing shop there. I found the shop and Maga, a heavy-set man in his forties, and introduced myself, explaining why I was there.

"*Yo te recuerdo. Tu eres La Catalina.*"

Much to my surprise, he remembered me, since I had no recollection of him. He said that Chino and Milicho were still in Atacames. Milicho had a bar and restaurant and was married to a Swiss woman and had a child, but she'd left a long time ago. Tarzan was living with his daughter Chita, who was now twenty years old. Jade had returned to France years before. My heart was pounding the whole time Maga talked at the possibility of seeing Milicho again. When I asked him why Milicho and Chino had not left Atacames, he said, "*Tu sabes como es la vida en Atacames.*"

Yes, I did remember what life was like there.

On the flight to Guayaquil, I prepared for the worst yet hoped for the best. I remembered the dreams I had so often in those first years, replaying in my head the scenes of my return, fine tuning them over and over, adding details and pacing, like a director building the drama. I pictured how I would enter the plaza, stop at the salon that Begner owned. It would be daytime, no one in there except a few old men drinking aguardiente, perhaps Don Rogelio, his eyes red and liquid from drink. I would walk in to gasps of "*¡Ay Catalina!* You've come back!" Then I would walk across the footbridge to find Milicho at his bar. After a moment of silence and recognition, we would embrace and cry and kiss.

I flew to Quito from Guayaquil then flew to Esmeraldas the next day. My arrival in Atacames was as easy as it was strange. I took a cab from the airport directly to the town, instead of riding in the open-air passenger truck from Esmeraldas like I did years before. As the taxi drove into the town, I tried to orient myself, but we were on a new road that bypassed the town plaza and went directly to the beach, past small hotels, bars and restaurants that had not existed in the 1970s.

New streets expanded the size of the town; the wooden footbridge was replaced by a curved metal bridge over the river, which had been redirected to make room for the road. Restaurants and small hotels lined the beach where once there was nothing but palm groves. When we arrived on the beach, the taxi driver asked some people where we could find Milicho.

"*No problemo,*" we were told. "*Él está en su bar,*" they said, motioning to his bar down the beach.

So he finally got his dream of having his own restaurant, I thought, something he had talked about so often. We pulled up next to a *jalapa* where tourists sat on stools made of palm tree stumps while salsa and Latin rap music blared from boom box speakers, the noise of the waves adding to the cacophony. It put me on edge. It was chaotic and unfamiliar, and not at all like the sweet moment of the return I had imagined.

The taxi driver got out and asked for Milicho. A man, gray in his hair, turned around and said, "*Soy el,* I am he."

As he spoke to the driver, I got out of the backseat and faced him. He looked like his older brother, no longer the sweet-faced boy I had known.

"*Hola, Milicho, soy Catalina.*"

"*¡Catalina!*" he said softly, slowly. We stood facing each other and embraced quickly, awkwardly. We did not fall into each other's arms or kiss like in my dreams. I asked how he was; he asked what I was doing there. He was neither icy nor warm, just disconnected. Somewhere behind that man's face was the boy I used to know, but I could not quite see him yet. Here was the moment I had been dreaming about for twenty years, and it was very, very uncomfortable.

"*¿Y tu mama, Señora Inez?*" I asked with apprehension. Is she still alive, I was asking behind my words.

"*Vive en el pueblo,*" he said. "*Venga,* I'll take you to her."

"Ok, I will take my bags to the hotel and be right back."

The taxi driver dropped me at the Arco Iris, a small hotel up the beach past where Señora Inez's casita had been. The hotel was perfect: funky, with greenery everywhere, little cabanas with hammocks in front, private bathrooms and air conditioning, away from the noise. There was even a pool where the palms once stood.

I checked in, then walked down the beach, my heart pounding, my body disoriented, back to Milicho's bar. He met me with a quick greeting, and we walked over the bridge to his mother's house. I asked questions, he said little in response. My Spanish felt awkward on my tongue, stumbling as I asked him about his life, his marriage, and what happened to us back then. He did not want to talk about any of it.

"Why do you want to know?" he asked. "*Así es la vida.* That's life. It happened." He did not want to connect with me at all, and I felt his discomfort.

**

When we arrived at his mother's house, a small casita on a side road in town, he called up to her. "*Mama, ven,* come see who is here!"

Señora Inez came out of the house and stood on the porch. "*¡Ay, Catalina! ¿Dónde has estado?*" she called to me, as if I had been away for a few days on a trip to Quito, not gone for twenty years.

I walked up the steps, and I was stunned. She looked just like Gramma Sadie, my father's mother who died in 1969. Same wide hips and sagging bosom inside a similar housedress. Her hair, her face, it was my grandmother's. How come I had never noticed that before? I looked up at Señora Inez and saw Gramma Sadie, widowed for thirty years, standing on the landing outside her apartment on Detroit Street in the Borscht Belt of Los Angeles. We called the street where so many grandparents — Yiddisha *bubbas* and *zedas* — lived out their years "Gramma Row," the slight aroma of onions cooked into the walls and linoleum floors.

I sat down at the bare wooden table while Señora Inez prepared her strong black coffee, some rolls, campesino cheese and papaya, as if we did this all the time. She was chatting away in her toothless, barely intelligible language. Coming back to Atacames made me realize we were not immortal. Milicho had aged; his sisters were grandmothers. Only Señora Inez remained the same, aged and ageless at the same time, as if time never passed.

Milicho left me with her and walked back to his bar. For the rest of the week, I tried to find him again, to talk to him, to connect as I'd dreamt we would, but it didn't happen.

I never saw him again.

CHAPTER 51:

REUNIONS

I went to the plaza, hoping to find my old friends. They were all there: Clodo, Chino, Tarzan, Pancho the baker, and Chino's sisters Zoila, Hilda, and Columbia. Don Rogelio, Chino's father, had died, as had Milicho's father. Everyone greeted me warmly with questions and hugs.

Chino and Clodo looked the same, just older; still thin, still with smoky eyes. Clodo had married a foreigner who went back to Europe, and Chino never married. Rumors abounded about them selling cocaine and weed and being lost *ladrones*, but none of that seemed true when I talked to them. Chino told me he had a business for a while selling coral jewelry and now had a bar on the plaza next to the old jugo man's place. Their lives had not changed that much, it seemed.

"Life here just is, a coming and going of negocio here and there," Clodo said. No one went to the beach or had much contact with the *locura*, the craziness of the tourists.

Chino said it was not true that he ripped me off. He knew I always believed he had stolen from me, and he was sorry I thought that. I was sorry too, although I knew it was true. Still, none of that mattered anymore.

As I sat on the bench in the plaza in front of the jugo place with Clodo and Chino, I regretted not coming back sooner. A man drove up the road on a motorbike and Chino flagged him down. As it got closer, I saw it was Lucho, and I froze with shock. All those years I'd focused only on the memories of Milicho and had erased Lucho completely from the story of my life there. In that moment, when he rode up on his motorbike, all of it came flooding back. My body flushed with heat, and I almost fell over from the rush of memory.

"*¡Ay, Catalina!*" he said with that familiar slow, deep voice. He looked the same, a little gray in the beard, but his body was strong and taut as ever. I spent a few hours at a bar on the plaza, chatting with Lucho and Phillip, a half gringo who lived off and on in Ecuador. He helped me translate the Costeño Spanish I could no longer understand that well. I could feel the heat rising in my body as I sat next to Lucho. I was still drawn to him, drawn to his intensity, and still shocked that I had so completely forgotten about him.

The next morning, I took a short jog along the wide, hard-packed sand at low tide and watched young men playing futbol. It was the same vision, only it wasn't Clodo and Milicho, but a younger set of boys. I sat down on an isolated stretch of beach away from the crowds and thought about what I had lost, what was not there anymore. I needed to sort out what was real and what was illusion, why I felt so much heart pain and joy at the same time. I had dropped back into a sliver of a life I once lived, even if just for a moment, but it was not the same. I wrote in my journal and let the tears come.

I only exist in the lives of the village when I am here. When I leave, I am not a part of it. When I show up again, I meld into the daily routine of the village, the canoes come in with the morning catch, the fishermen wave to me as they pass by. I walk across the footbridge as I did a thousand times, and I am simultaneously now and twenty years before and twenty years from now. Time means nothing, the life of the village goes on whether I am in it or not. I sit with Chino and Lucho on the bench in the plaza, across from the jugo man's shop window, but the jugo man is no longer there. He is dead, the window and the shop still stand, empty. I walk up the beach where Señora Inez's house once stood in palm groves that were cut to make room for a road and hotels. I walk to her house on an unfamiliar street in town. She greets me, Aye, Catalina, where have you been? Come inside, I made coffee, and I step into her house and sit at the table. It could be now, it could be twenty years ago, it could be twenty years from now. There is no past or future when I am in the village; there is only the present. I sip the strong coffee and take a bit of the hard roll and a bit of salty cheese. I exist in that place, in that moment, and in a few days, I will be gone again, and my life there will disappear again.

On my way back toward the bridge, I ran into Cabeza Loco, who said life was better there now. There was more to do, more businesses, more money to be made. No one was getting rich, no one was getting very far, but they were doing better. The children were healthier and better educated. We walked down the beach together, smoked *un pito*, and talked of old times. He was one of *los encarcelados*, jailed in Ambato with Milicho, and we laughed about how crazy that all had been.

I did not want to remember that Atacames was a tourist town, that the people wanted development, hotels, roads, cars, money. They wanted plastics and washing machines, electricity and toilets, and they got what they wanted, for better or worse. The town I once knew was unrecognizable; its streets filled with t-shirt shops with plastic beach toys hanging from the tin roofs. The beach was crowded with tourists, with more noise and garbage, and lined with hotels and restaurants and even swimming pools. The gorgeous Atacames beach was now trashed. They wanted this to happen, but I wanted it to stay undeveloped, idyllic in its poverty and simplicity. I already had the things they desired, the conveniences of modern life I took for granted but they needed so desperately.

And yet, it was striking how poor so many people still were. Many houses were made of guadua bamboo with muddy concrete floors. Some people had no bathroom; Señora Inez had no shower. Some had small refrigerators and stoves, and cold drinks were available in the shops. But the electricity turned off during the night, and preservation of food was still difficult. Some of the streets were paved with cement block but most were not, and when it rained hard all the streets turned into a muddy, sandy mess. No one wore nice clothes except to church, where the women wore costume jewelry and floral print dresses or tops. I laughed thinking how well my mother's costume jewelry business would do there.

The food was fresh and wonderful, just as before. I was reminded how the dishes were prepared, dishes that for some silly reason I'd never tried to make in the years since. I remembered how to plop plátanos verdes in boiling water for soup or boil sweet *maduros* mashed with milk, or bake them on charcoal like potatoes, or smash fried plátanos into thick *patacones*, or make *chifles*, fried chips. And the fish! There was *pescado asado*, fish wrapped in aluminum and baked on coal until it was crisp on the outside, or marinated with salt, garlic, pepper and lemons and fried or steamed. There was ceviche, fresh seafood marinated in lemon and cilantro, and spicy fish stew. All *delicioso como siempre,* delicious as always.

The word spread that I had come back, and people called out to me, "*¡Ay Catalina! ¡El tiempo que ha pasada!*" I was surprised that so many people recognized me, and some told me they remembered me for my smile. My memory was terrible; people's faces were familiar, but I remembered so few of their names. One man here said it best when I was lamenting that I should have come back earlier, that I had forgotten so much. He said life is forever ahead of us, *siempre adelante.*

I met up with Chino's sisters Columbia, Zoila and Hilda at Columbia's house. Begner was there, talking of old times and sharing the latest news. We reminisced about the time the muchachos were in jail in Ambato, of Milicho, of babies and the passage of time. I was struck by how many children they had, with different men or consecutive husbands, each with five, six, or seven kids.

How could they all be so fertile and me not? I mused silently while they chatted around me. I wondered if I would have ended up with a bunch of kids had I stayed. *Maybe it was something in the water!* I laughed to myself at that one.

I left after a lovely lunch and took a walk to find my old house, the one I lived in with Milicho.

But the casita was no longer there, disappeared into the fog of a dream.

CHAPTER 52:

LUCHO

The following evening, I swung in my hammock at the hotel, waiting for Tarzan to take me dancing. He was late and I was not sure he was coming. There were no lights at night and sadly the beach had become a bit dangerous.

I was reminded of the first time Milicho came to the travelers' house on the beach to bring me to the dance in town. Paula, *La Chilena*, had dressed me up. That was our first date, which began the whole love affair. Now once again I was waiting on the beach to go dancing. This time Milicho would not be there, but Lucho would.

Earlier that morning, Lucho had taken me on his motorbike to Muisne, a small town south of Atacames. Muisne looked like Atacames used to, with palm groves and palapas. We ate fresh fish and *ceviche de camarones* right on the beach, walked along the sand, went in and out of the water, and talked of old times. He said he thought of me often and had a lot of regret for the way he had treated me. He reminded me of the letters he wrote to me after I went home. It was Lucho who wanted me to come back, not Milicho. It was Lucho who wrote letters to me for months, declaring his love for me and telling me about his life. I had no memory of them, of reading them or answering them, and I was afraid to ask him if I responded. I did not remember why or when the letters stopped coming. It terrified me that I had no memory of any of that. I could barely remember the details of our time together, only the hurt, which by then was only part of a larger hurt of a life falling apart.

Lucho expressed no regret for having cheated on Gloria at the time, or for not telling me about her in the beginning. She was understand-ably jealous of his meanderings and gave him a lot of grief. They had broken up when he got together with me. They eventually got married and had two more kids. All I could think about was how attractive he still was to me, even now as adults, twenty years later. I could feel myself once again falling into that old craziness of desire, with little regard for the consequences. We came back to my hotel in the afternoon and made love until he had to leave.

Now it was evening, and I was tired of waiting for Tarzan. I grabbed a flashlight and headed down the beach and crossed the bridge to town. The disco was not at all like the salon I used to go to. This was outside with stump seats and tables around the edge of the dance floor, with a good sound system, not the scratchy boom box sitting on Begner's bar. The music was a modern, fast mix of merengue and rock, though occasionally they played salsa and cumbia for us old-timers. There were mostly men sitting and drinking, and the whole scene came back to me, of hanging out with los muchachos who drank too much while the women stayed home in *la casa* with the kids.

I danced with Clodo for a while and then, when Lucho and I danced, the attraction was so strong I was out of breath. It started to rain, hard, as we were dancing in the open patio. Pretty soon we were the only ones out there, laughing and getting drenched, with all eyes on us. He told me that people were watching because I danced like a Latina. We walked back to the beach in a tremendous aguacera, stepping gingerly in the muddy sand. We arrived at my hotel just as the lights in the whole town went out for the third night in a row. It was so dark I could not see him in the bed, and our lovemaking was intense and incredibly powerful.

Lucho talked about wishing he did not have *compromisos*, commitments, his wife and kids. If he didn't, he thought we could be together. I knew that wasn't true; our passion felt more than just sexual but it was not real. I merely craved that intensity, something I wanted back in my life, and was willing to play with fire because I was only there for a moment. I did not have to think about what damage I would cause, and I ignored feelings of guilt for making love to a married man.

The next morning, I met up with Chino and Tarzan. We climbed a steep hill overlooking a gorgeous view of the area. On one side were camarones pools, shrimp farms similar to rice paddies, and green mountains; on the other side, Atacames and the beach. It could be the view from Pacific Palisades or Malibu, except for the bamboo huts and banana trees.

After taking in the spectacular vistas, we climbed down and bought fish, plátanos and onions, *aguacate*, and *limón* and enjoyed a delicious Atacamanian fish fry at a comedor. Chino, Clodo, Tarzan and me, together again. They were all the same, only quieter, and a lot less loco. Perhaps I had changed as well, perhaps I was not as crazy anymore, but how could I explain my behavior with Lucho? I could feel the tropical heat of lust taking over my senses once again.

I went to church in the afternoon for the First Communion of some of the children, including Lucho's daughter and nephew and some kids in Chino's family. There were some twenty children or so, all dressed in starched white little-man shirts and full-skirted white dresses. It was a big deal, with all the godparents, *las comadres* and *los compadres*, in town for parties afterward. I felt uncomfortable standing on the side outside of the church, somehow a part of it and a stranger at the same time. Lucho was with Gloria, their three kids, and their extended family. I watched as they piled into a pickup and went off to his house for a fiesta, feeling ashamed that I was complicit in his infidelity. I was unmoored by the whole thing.

The next day, my last day, I stayed on the beach, swam in the pool, played in the strong waves, and rested in the hammock. As I was leaving to cross into town, Lucho appeared looking for me. We spent the next few hours walking on the beach. He was very drunk, so we walked until he came down a bit, and then we went into town to meet up with Chino and Poncho Figueroa and Tarzan, all of them drinking trago and beer until midnight, before the lights went out.

There was a moment there of stillness, of fullness, as if no time had passed. I felt a warmth for those friends of mine. We could only imagine what changes we had all been through, how time had impacted us, yet sitting there, we looked the same to each other, even if we felt older to ourselves. We raised our glasses and toasted to the past and laughed, *como siempre.*

Lucho and I walked back up the beach to my hotel after the lights went out. The sky was filled with stars, and the town was pitch black, country dark. We made love by candlelight, our bodies making shadows on the curtains.

"*Oye, gringita, te quiero. Por cierto. Te quiero.*" He said he loved me for certain.

I knew better than to believe that, but it did feel as if my open heart had been left on this beach years before and closed up after I left. After one week I could feel it opening again, and it was not just Lucho, but the huge feelings I had for the people there, the large extended families, everyone knowing each other, for better or worse, caring for each other, the whole village caring for the children, the warmth and *cariño* that was their way of life.

Lucho said, "*Tienes el corazón de una Costeña,*" that I had the heart of a local, that I was not a gringa. Perhaps he was right: I found La Catalina's heart again that week, still beating, still alive.

I left the next day as I said I would. I said goodbye to Señora Inez, to the muchachos and the sisters. I did not see Milicho to say goodbye or take a photo; he was not a part of that week. We were strangers, our connection in the past. Strange how things happen.

Así es la vida.

CHAPTER 53:

STORIES

As the years passed, my memory of that time drifted into the haze, and I began writing down the stories that came to me, grabbing them like trying to catch a dream. I filled notebooks with stories, reflections and dreams.

The woman lay quiet on the table, the paper gown too small to cover her, needles making a straight path from above her navel downward, a few pinning down her feet and hands. She lay still, deepening her breath, adjusting her shoulder back and down in yoga resting pose. She did not sleep, but fell into a deeper state of relaxation, the better to let the needles do their work, opening the channels of energy in her womb.

She longed for heat, that internal combustion in her groin, the flush of warmth on the way to orgasm. An orgasm seemed too distant a goal. Now she merely wished for a little heat, and perhaps some moisture inside. She had been in this cold state for so long. Funny how suddenly the heat went away, from one day to the next it seemed.

She no longer felt the ping of menstruation in her ovaries or the fire of cramps knocking her over in a bath of red pain. She did not miss that. But when that went away, it took with it everything else, like the tsunami wave gathering up all life and sucking it out to sea in the blink of an eye, leaving her cold and empty, the fire gone out.

She thought about the intensity of earlier times. Oh, the passion, the lust, the single-minded urge to push her hips up against another. That drive had ruled her for so long, the current of sexual desire moving inside her constantly, clouding her judgment, overriding reason. She thought of all the boys in her life and how far away she was from her lust, now so completely transformed by time, and perhaps by wisdom.

Milicho, Milicho, she sighed to herself, in partial dream state. Her body flat and still, the needles on her belly rising softly up, down, up with her breath. How crazy I was for you, she thought. We made love on the riverbank, in the wet sand, flies buzzing around our wetness. It didn't matter, so much wetness, heat inside and out. I came inside myself just by touching your skin, that was enough. And it was not only you: there were others, so many crazy moments, so many times I did anything I could to feed that fire inside my groin. I was insane. But Milicho, you were different. No, I was different. I was in love.

She wondered if she would ever again experience the purity of those original feelings. Probably not, she thought, stretching her toes now, clenching and unclenching her fists. She sighed, now completely back to the surface. Just as well, she thought. I would be happy with just a little heat, but I could do without the heartbreak.

CHAPTER 54:

DREAMS OF SEÑORA INEZ

Thirty years after I left Atacames, I lived for a few years on a farm in Northern California with sheep as my constant companions. My writing room overlooked the pasture where the ewes grazed and nursed their lambs. They often bleated at me impatiently when the grass was not enough to quell their hunger. I sat in that room and let the memories of my time in another rural life, a life closer to nature, come into my mind. I closed my eyes and fell into a dream about my time in the palm groves with Señora Inez.

Señora Inez, have you come to me again, to try to teach me? Are your teeth clucking sounds of impatience disguised as Brown Mama sheep's yells? Now you have come to me in a different place, another place of ocean, of river and rain. Once again, I am living closer to the earth, in a place quiet enough for me to think the birds are too loud. You were gentle in your lessons, softly sighing "¡Ay, Catalina!" under your breath, your head shaking in wonderment at how I could possibly survive in the world with so few skills, so little awareness. Perhaps now you think that screaming at me, with a long tongue out, is what is needed to get my attention.

Did I learn anything back then? Did I have any honor? I was so hungry for the boys I embarrassed myself with my wants, needs, lusts, and my incessant questions. Better to have shut up and paid more attention to the ocean waves, the breezes in the palms, even the tiny geckos that had wisdom to share if only I'd listened. You waited on me, my young eyes not able to see past my own needs, my arms not strong enough to haul the bucket of well water up without help. Your daughters made fun of me and mimicked my Spanish. You merely clucked your tongue, shook your head and sighed, "¡Ay Catalina!"

You took care of me, treated me as Number One Daughter, better than your own. Was it because your son loved me, and I loved him? You wanted me to be your family, marry your son. Or was it because you feared I would not survive without such care, my own mother too far away to help? You poured gasoline on my hair when I got lice, put a poultice on my staph-infected feet. You worried that my eyes would be damaged by too much reading. You treated me like a daughter-in-law of noble birth, with hands too delicate for the real work of women.

You were of service to me when it should have been the other way around. Was it the gringa in me you served, the gringa I could never not be no matter how hard I tried? I learned the language, got the accent down, listened to the singing phrases and repeated them back perfectly like a parrot. I studied and practiced how the women danced, how they held their shoulders, moving only their hips. But I never stopped assuming I could walk anywhere I wanted with anyone I wanted, go up the beach to smoke a joint with the muchachos, swim in the ocean in a two-piece bathing suit. I was still the tourist, my billfold of traveler's checks unused in my backpack, a constant reminder that I was not, and never would be, there forever.

I remember when you started mumbling the words mal ojo, clicking your tongue as you walked by me. This was the cause of my dysentery, infections, lice, and later, measles, you said. You were trying to tell me that my sickness was deeper than stomach bugs. I was out of balance, my immune system depleted by pollution, chemicals, smog, hubris, and drugs.

How could I have listened to what you were offering when my vision was fogged, my hearing dulled, my attention misplaced? I refused to look beyond the limits of my sight. You offered me a glimpse of the unseen, an opportunity to be touched by spirit, to witness and experience that which is beyond our usual knowing. You rubbed the egg over my skin and brought in the spirits to help me, to right the imbalance, heal me of the toxins. I was made well for a little while but my resistance and ignorance were too great and so the spirits left.

When the dysentery returned, I thought the healer had failed. "No te vayas," you said. "Don't go. You won't be healed. They don't know how to heal you." After my bout with measles, my body was intact, thanks to you, but my heart was broken and I left, again, this time for good. I did get healthy again, physically. But it was your teachings and your love that healed my heart.

CHAPTER 55:

LIMINALIDAD

For years, Atacames continued to have a mystical place in my mind. It was a place of intense emotional memories, drawing me back again and again. Atacames was aguaceras, banana trees and aquamarine ocean water, luscious mangos and wet kisses from warm, honey-skinned boys. Atacames was longing and searching for commitment. It was difficult to find those things in the tropics where the ground shifts, the trees have shallow roots, the sand washes the paths away, and the rivers change course.

I tried to feel secure in Atacames, but the foundations of my life there were unreliable, and no one could be completely trusted. The boy I loved slipped away and my other lovers lied to me. Atacames broke my heart. These truths I came to understand only after I got out from under the weight of that place, the energy of Atacames eventually dissipating enough to let me see it from a distance. I had been in a power struggle with it, trying to make a home there, but I was battered, depleted. I left before it killed me, yet I longed to go back there for years.

When I first returned home, I was physically present but in an emotional state of liminality, neither fully done with Ecuador nor fully in my life in Los Angeles. It was as if my soul was living in between two places. Eventually I lost the unsettled dismay at being back in the States and made the commitment to being here, to getting involved in my world, not as a tourist in another culture. I bought a house on Venice Beach and created a life full of friends, family, serious work, social justice activism and music. I chose work that put me face to face with my ignorance, naïveté and privilege. I became a public defender, representing poor people in criminal court.

When I came home and could speak and understand Spanish, a whole different part of Los Angeles opened up to me, as if I could suddenly hear it for the first time. I spoke Spanish to my clients from Mexico, Guatemala, and El Salvador, who were always surprised by my non-gringo accent. I had conversations with the Latino people around me, the shopkeepers and housekeepers, gardeners and workers, bailiffs and lawyers, and it enriched my life in that bilingual city.

Ever since, I have lived with one foot embedded in the mud of Third World countries, involved in the struggles to improve the lives of the people who left those places to seek safety in mine. I never let go of the lessons learned: that the world is a big place, filled with people who are mostly not white, not rich, yet whose lives are far richer and more amazing than I ever thought. The experiences I had there helped strip away the layers of arrogance I carried just by virtue of where and what I came from. Every step in that journey was a step from knowing everything to knowing nothing, from pride to humility, from obliviousness to awareness.

I carry a little lump of Ecuador inside me still, like a beating heart. It sits nestled in my mind and body, a pacemaker of sorts, sending out vibrations of memory. My Latina persona is tucked inside there, coming out when I dance salsa or chat in Spanish. All these years later, I can dip into this jar of tropical juice that tastes like guanabana and smells like coconut. It is the softness of the tropics, the swaying of palm fronds in warm breezes, that sends me to that place. I go there when I am in Kauai or Louisiana or Mexico, when it is hot and humid and the fragrance of the plumeria and hibiscus come into my window at night, and I remember my time there.

I no longer live abroad in a foreign land.

The foreign land, the memories of Ecuador, of Atacames, of the Gringo Trail, live inside of me.

EPILOGUE

Years after this journey, I wrote down the stories I could remember. I kept my diaries from that time close, but I did not read them. I wanted to put down everything I could remember first. My memories of that time were like dreams popping out of the fog and floating away, little filaments of scenes I saw myself in but did not really remember how I felt when I was in them. It was in the diaries that I would find the feelings and thoughts. Somehow the diaries were an offering: here, here is your memory, here is how you felt. If I did not put that in the stories, the memoir would be nothing more than travelogue.

I finally read the diaries some forty years after my journey. I typed them up verbatim, laying bare whatever truths there were, good and bad, remembered or not, and melded them together with the stories written later. The stories are all here, from the twenty-something girl and what was important to her to the stories written by the woman in the subsequent decades of life, in a layered journey of memory itself.

Reading the diaries so many years later was a shock and a revelation. Strangely, some of the stories I remembered as key, intense moments were nowhere to be found or barely mentioned in my diaries. Did they not happen, or were they not important at the time? There were descriptions and names of lots of people I met and befriended, stayed with and traveled with, and I was astonished at how little I remembered about any of those people. Memory is a fascinating thing: Sometimes we don't remember what happened, but rather what we told people happened. Sometimes the truth is too painful or shameful or dull, so we tell the story we want or the story we can handle. Eventually the truth fades, and we are left with only the story, a story we let define ourselves, for better or worse.

The diaries document my insistence on traveling without spending money, a hippie of sorts refusing the trappings of wealth. It's as if I wanted a life that was more difficult. I wanted to be part of a struggle, but I had none, so I invented it to give my life more romance. I made a choice to be uncomfortable, to play at scarcity, pretend at poverty. I did not need to buy a pound of pot in Colombia and risk prison by taping it to my stomach and crossing the border to make $200. I could have called home for cash at any time. Part of that was coming from the culture and politics of my Berkeley days, when we lived communally, tried to live simply, grow our own vegetables and make our own bread. It was also the culture of the Gringo Trail, where for many on it, spending as little as possible meant traveling as long as possible. I wanted to be part of that tribe. I wanted to travel close to the ground, to learn about the cultures and experience them, rather than float above them in hotels and tour buses. I wanted to be with people who had no idea who I was, what my life was like before, who my family was. I got to let it all be unknown and spend a few years being a completely different person.

The most wonderfully surprising gift of the diaries is learning who the girl who went on that journey really was. The story I told for years was that of a sexually naïve and shy young woman who did not relate to men very well and stayed detached and defensive to keep from getting hurt. Then my story is one of meeting a boy, falling in love, getting my heart broken and never falling in love again. I realize now that this was hogwash. The diaries revealed a completely different person, and I barely recognized her. Who was that girl? Yes, she was thoughtful, intellectual, Berkeley-educated, with astute observations about the world she was traveling through. But she was also someone who gathered friends wherever she went and was fearless and adventurous every step of the way.

That young woman fell into bed as easily and often as eating tortillas and campesino cheese. It was the "Fuck Tour of Latin America," starting in Mexico and rolling through Central America to South America, leaving sexual and emotional detritus all along the Gringo Trail, ending up in a wild telenovela in Atacames. I was shocked, not only by how promiscuous that girl was, but more significantly, by how little memory I had of much of this wild behavior.

Why would I remember only the boy I loved and lost, rather than all the others I toyed with so nonchalantly then promptly forgot? I crafted a scenario where I am the one tossed aside by my one true love, but I blocked the memory of the girl who hurt others, who played with men, and had a good time doing it. It was not Milicho who needed to be forgiven for leaving me. If anyone needed to be forgiven for such bad behavior, it was me.

Perhaps it was more useful to create a story of the heartbroken, love-lorn innocent, rather than the story of a young woman who barreled her way into worlds she did not know very well, wanting to suck every drop of experience from the people she encountered, sleep with young men she would say goodbye to the next day, ask too many questions and stare too intently. Perhaps Señora Inez was right: I did have mal ojo, oblivious to the effect I was having on others. Or perhaps even that was just hogwash, and the truth is, I was a young hippie tourist gallivanting about in a strange and interesting place.

Perhaps I had been mourning the loss of something that was never real, that holy grail of falling in love, with all the desperate, intense desires that it entails. Perhaps that young-girl passion was just what it was, but the real, useful, purposeful, meaningful state of love is what I felt for the partner I met twenty-five years after leaving Atacames, and for my friends and my family and my dog and my cats, and even the crazy squirrel who steals my figs.

Now I can let go of the hurt I carried because of lost love and come to understand that I was loved, and that I loved deeply as well. I loved those people, all of them, the muchachos, the women of the village, the Brazilians and Chilenos and Argentinian students and artists, the fishermen and campesinos, the young boys sitting on the roof of buses, the fruit sellers and the fishermen, even the bowler-hatted Bolivian women and the scowling Peruvian shopkeepers.

Writing this book allowed me to let go of the old story of loss and heartbreak and embrace the true story, of a vibrant, curious young woman who brought what she learned on the Gringo Trail into a life of caring and commitment; who was not a heartbroken victim who could never risk loving again; who continued to have lovers and sexual escapades and hot foreplay on the dance floor; who never let go of the passion, fierceness and cumbia of Atacames.

A woman who never let go of La Catalina.

**

THIS IS WHAT I KNOW ABOUT LOVE

It is small sometimes, imperceivable often.
It lives in small places, and it sometimes hides.
It is in the small glance of dark eyes from a Guatemalan
Indian baby wrapped like a burrito on his mother's back.
It is in the deep red, yellow and pink flowers of the
coleus hedges that line the streets of Cuernavaca.
It is underneath the folds of the Quiché woman's huipil where
an infant suckles on her brown breast, while the woman
offers carrots and tomatoes piled on her blanket.
It offered itself to me in every bite of strange new fruits, of chirimoya
and guanabana, the luscious green pulp dribbling down my chin.
It offered itself to me in the simple acts of generosity, giving me
seats on crowded buses, in the waves of hands of countless smil-
ing children, their teeth whitened by chewing coconut meat.
It was not in the offerings of sex from desperate young men.
That was not love they offered, and it was not love I gave in return.
It is in the dusty roads and dirt floor cafés and freshly
made tortillas and smells of roasting corn.
It is in the deep blue skies, intense sunrises and glorious sunsets.
It is in the joy of astounding landscapes, ancient farms using ancient
practices, patches of corn and vegetables growing up the sides of
mountains like quilts made of multi-colored fabric, dotted with farmers
wrapped in the bright reds, oranges and yellows of their woven ponchos.

It is in every market filled with fruits and pota-
toes, in every dirt-floored home.
It is in something so simple as a good, clean
bed and a cup of strong coffee.
It was not only in the kisses and touch of the choco-
late-skinned lovers, but in the breakfasts of eggs and
baked plátanos offered by their mothers and sisters.
It was in the embrace of the women who healed me,
washed me, fed me, and taught me to dance.
It is in every village where I rested, every stream
and well where I washed my body.
It is in the people who had nothing but gave me everything I needed,
who offered far more than I was able to give in return.
I was nurtured and kept safe by strangers who came into my life for brief
moments on a moving journey, often in cold, uncomfortable places.
I now see the beauty and feel the warmth of those moments.
It was what I was searching for and what I found
in ways I never expected or imagined.

ACKNOWLEDGMENTS

This book was birthed out of the many writing groups and classes I attended over the years. I want to thank Deena Metzger for starting me on this journey of creative and meaningful storytelling. Sitting with her in circle in Topanga Canyon gave me permission to take my writing seriously. There are others who helped me craft these stories along the way: Carolyn Brigit Flynn and Dorothy Randall Gray, and the wonderful community of writers of Drop In and Write. I want to especially thank my amazing and talented writing teacher, Wendy Hammers, for giving me back my humor, and Suzanne Weertz for helping me turn a jumble of stories into a book. Thanks, also, to my editor Corey Stewart and the team at DartFrog Books, who pushed the book out into the world.

ABOUT THE AUTHOR

Cathy Dreyfuss was born in New York City and raised in Los Angeles. She received a BA from UC Berkeley and a law degree from USC. She represented indigent criminal defendants and immigrants for many years in the offices of the Public Defender, the ACLU of Southern California, Northern California Innocence Project and Immigrant Defenders Law Center. She was also active in the National Lawyers Guild throughout her career. Cathy began writing personal stories and essays while working as an attorney. She recently left the courtroom for the storytelling stage, performing in Tasty Words and JAM Creative productions. Her piece, *Black Bread and Herring*, was published in the anthology *Rings of Kindness* in 2023. Cathy still travels the world, swimming in every sea and ocean she can, but always returns to her home on Venice Beach to host dinners, music jams and dance parties in her garden. *Tripping over Love on the Gringo Trail* is her first book.

www.ingramcontent.com/pod-product-compliance
Lightning Source LLC
Chambersburg PA
CBHW020233130626
46549CB00005B/1865